STEP UP TO IELTS

VANESSA JAKEMAN and **CLARE McDOWELL**

Personal Study Book

CAMBRIDGE
UNIVERSITY PRESS

PUBLISHED BY THE PRESS SYNDICATE OF THE UNIVERSITY OF CAMBRIDGE
The Pitt Building, Trumpington Street, Cambridge, United Kingdom

CAMBRIDGE UNIVERSITY PRESS
The Edinburgh Building, Cambridge CB2 2RU, UK
40 West 20th Street, New York, NY 10011–4211, USA
477 Williamstown Road, Port Melbourne, VIC 3207, Australia
Ruiz de Alarcón 13, 28014 Madrid, Spain
Dock House, The Waterfront, Cape Town 8001, South Africa

http://www.cambridge.org

First published 2004

Printed in the United Kingdom at the University Press, Cambridge

Text typeface NewsGothic 9/12pt System QuarkXpress® [kamae]

A catalogue record for this book is available from the British Library

ISBN 0 521 53297 3 Student's Book
ISBN 0 521 53298 1 Student's Book with Answers
ISBN 0 521 53301 5 Teacher's Book
ISBN 0 521 53299 X Personal Study Book
ISBN 0 521 53300 7 Personal Study Book with Answers
ISBN 0 521 53303 1 Set of 2 audio cassettes
ISBN 0 521 54470 X Set of 2 audio CDs
ISBN 0 521 53302 3 Self-study pack

Cover design by Tim Elcock

Produced by Kamae Design, Oxford.

UNIT 9 *The driving force*

Vocabulary	Grammar	Writing
Describing cars	*Because* and *because of*	Collective nouns
Compound nouns	Linking words	Describing a table

 UNIT 10 *The silver screen*

Vocabulary	Grammar	Writing
Film words	Tense revision	Autobiography
		Biography

 UNIT 11 *The written word*

Vocabulary	Grammar	Writing
Describing books and journals	Adverbs	Using adverbs and adjectives
	Collocation	Letter writing

 UNIT 12 *Down to Earth*

Vocabulary	Grammar	Writing
Talking about rubbish	Verbs followed by prepositions	Balancing your views

 UNIT 13 *Safe as houses*

Vocabulary	Grammar	Writing
Describing houses	Linking and reference words	Making a concession
Crossword	Expressing purpose with '*in order to*'	

 UNIT 14 *On the face of it*

Vocabulary	Grammar	Writing
Adjective formation	Phrasal verbs	Describing what people do

 UNIT 15 *As far as I can see*

Vocabulary	Grammar	Writing
Abbreviations	The future	Checking for reference and
Reference word plus noun formation		tense error

 UNIT 16 *Mother tongue*

Vocabulary	Grammar	Writing
Word puzzle	Adverbs ending in -*ly*	Linking words
Singular and plural meanings	Indirect questions	Main ideas

Take a break

Describing hobbies and interests

1 Which of the following activities are sports and which are hobbies?
Write them in the appropriate column below. Ignore column 2 for now.

> ~~sailing~~   reading   golf   gardening   rock climbing   chess   judo
> kite flying   badminton   dancing   painting   horse riding

1 sports	2 type of people
sailing	brave

1 hobbies	2 type of people

2 What type of people are good at these activities? Choose an adjective
from the box below and write it in column 2 above. You may choose more
than one adjective or add your own.

> patient   flexible   quiet   adventurous   intelligent   thoughtful
> brave   energetic   athletic   accurate   careful   artistic   strong
> musical   fit

3 Complete this table. Add your own three favourite hobbies to the list.

You have to be	.........fit.........	to be good at	horse riding.
	....		....
	....		....
	....		....

Sporting words

4 Match the sports with the equipment.

sport	equipment
1 cycling	a boat
2 table tennis	b goggles
3 tennis	c pieces
4 swimming	d clubs
5 chess	e bicycle
6 golf	f racket
7 rowing	g skates
8 ice hockey	h bat

GRAMMAR

Adjectives ending in -ing and -ed

1 **Look at the box of verbs and complete the sentences using an appropriate present participle (-*ing*) or past participle (-*ed*). Sometimes more than one answer is possible.**

amaze   bore   enchant   exhaust   fascinate   interest   irritate   worry

Example: I've been working for over twelve hours and now I feel completely ...*exhausted*... .

1 The film had some .... underwater shots of sharks and stingrays.
2 Our flight was delayed by six hours so we waited at the airport. I have never felt so .... in all my life.
3 Dr Asquith is a great lecturer because he's such an .... man.
4 The mosquitoes are extremely .... this evening.
5 Teenagers often find 19th-century novels .... because they are difficult to read.
6 The magic scenes in the film were quite ....
7 We were absolutely .... by the sharks at the aquarium.
8 You look .... to death. Whatever is the matter?

Present simple and present continuous

GRAMMAR

Ping **comes** from Beijing in China. She**'s learning** English because she wants to go to London to study engineering.

Present simple
For habits and states.

Present continuous
For actions taking place at the time of speaking or writing.

2 **Complete the sentences using either a present simple or a present continuous form of the verb in brackets.**

Example: The operation ...*is taking place*... right now. The patient is still in the operating theatre. (take place)

1 This phone .... well at the moment. (not work) Can I call you back later?
2 I'm at home all day but my husband isn't. He always .... to the office on Saturday. (go)
3 Good morning! I .... money for the Red Cross. Would you like to donate something? (collect)
4 Hello! I .... to get hold of Mr Jones. Do I have the right number? (try)
5 I .... a course in First Aid at the Red Cross because I .... it for my job. (attend) (need)
6 I .... from Japan. I was born in Tokyo in 1988. (come)
7 What .... ? I told you not to touch the wet paint! (you/do)
8 My grandmother .... to ski, which is quite brave at her age. (learn)

Writing a thank-you letter to someone you know

1 Complete the letter below with an appropriate word in each space.

2 Complete the notes in the margin at (b) and (c) to summarise the purpose of the second and third paragraphs.

Dear Aunty Lucy,

I'm (1) .... to thank you very much for the lovely present you (2) .... me for my birthday. A new tennis (3) .... is just what I wanted and I know I'm going to enjoy (4) .... with it. Maybe it will help to improve my game!

In addition to your present, I also (5) .... a computerised chess game. When you make a mistake, the computer (6) .... to you and actually says: "That was a bad move!" We were all very (7) .... by it because it's very funny. I haven't managed to (8) .... the computer yet, but I will keep trying.

I hope you and Uncle Fred are both well and (9) .... yourselves in your new house. We are all looking forward to (10) .... you in the holidays. Thanks again for the lovely present.

Best wishes,

Bernard

a) Identifies the present and thanks her.

b) ....
....
....

c) ....
....
....

Introduction and tone

3 Now write the opening paragraph of a letter to:

1 a friend who has sent you a present for your birthday.
2 a relative who has invited you to an important family celebration.
3 someone who has advertised a room to let in his house.

Dear ...

WORD LIST

academic *adj* (p 10) related to education, schools, universities, etc.

accident *n* (p 11) something bad which happens that is not intended and which causes injury or damage

accommodation *n* (p 13) a place where you live or stay

achievement *n* (p 13) when you succeed in doing something good, usually by working hard

activity *n* (p 6) something which you do for enjoyment, especially an organized event

approach *n* (p 12) a way of doing something

appropriate *adj* (p 8) suitable or right for a particular situation or person

basic *adj* (p 8) being the main or most important part of something

career *n* (p 13) a job that you do for a long period of your life and that gives you the chance to move to a higher position and earn more money

challenge *n* (p 12) something that is difficult and that tests someone's ability or determination

common *adj* (p 12) belonging to or shared by two or more people or things

competition *n* (p 12) an organized event in which people try to win a prize by being the best, fastest, etc

computer *n* (p 6) an electronic machine that can store and arrange large amounts of information

contribution *n* (p 13) something that you do to help produce or develop something, or to help make something successful: *She has made a major contribution to our work.*

conversation *n* (p 8) a talk between two or more people, usually an informal one

development *n* (p 13) when someone or something grows or changes and becomes more advanced: *There have been some major developments in technology recently.*

disappointing *adj* (p 13) making you feel disappointed, i.e. unhappy because something or someone was not as good as you hoped or expected, or because something did not happen: *a disappointing performance/result*

effect *n* (p 13) a change, reaction, or result that is caused by something

emphasis *n* (p 7) particular importance or attention that you give to something

equipment *n* (p 8) the things that are used for a particular activity or purpose

facility *n* (p 13) a place where a particular activity happens: *a new medical facility*

favourite *adj* (p 9) Your favourite person or thing is the one that you like best.

individual *adj* (p 12) given to or relating to one particular person or thing: *We deal with each case on an individual basis.*

introduction *n* (p 10) the first time someone experiences something

listen *v* (p 8) to give attention to someone or something in order to hear them

machine *n* (p 12) a piece of equipment with moving parts that uses power to do a particular job

marvellous *adj* (p 11) extremely good

membership *n* (p 12) the state of belonging to a group or an organization

minimum *adj* (p 8) The minimum amount of something is the smallest amount that is allowed, needed, or possible.

national *adj* (p 13) relating to the whole of a country

opposite *adj* (p 7) in a position facing something or someone but on the other side: *on the opposite page*

ordinary *adj* (p 8) not special, different, or unusual in any way

organization *n* (p 13) an official group of people who work together for the same purpose

separate *adj* (p 13) different

standard *n* (p 13) a level of quality, especially a level that is acceptable: *a high standard of service*

strength *n* (p 12) when someone or something is strong: *upper-body strength*

successful *adj* (p 13) achieving what you want to achieve: *If the operation is successful, she should be walking within a few months.*

training *n* (p 11) the process of learning the skills you need to do a particular job or activity

website *n* (p 12) an area on the Web (= computer information system) where information about a particular subject, organization, etc can be found

worldwide *adj,adv* (p 13) in all parts of the world

UNIT 2

What's on the menu?

VOCABULARY

Names of food and drink

1 Add as many items as you can to the categories of food and drink.

dairy products	vegetables	fruit	drinks
cheese	potatoes	apples	milk

Describing portions of food

2 Match the food and drink on the left with a word from each box to make a food phrase.

Example: a ....*slice*.... of ..*bread*..

slice
bowl
carton
plate
piece
packet
bar

1 a .... of ....

2 a .... of ....

3 a .... of ....

4 a .... of ....

5 a .... of ....

6 a .... of ....

bread
cake
chocolate
crisps
milk
pasta
rice

3 Use one of the words from the box to build up each phrase from exercise 2.

Example: *a slice of crusty bread*

milk	steamed	fresh	crusty	potato	chocolate

9

GRAMMAR

Countable and uncountable nouns

1 Complete each sentence using a word from the table.

With countable nouns we use:	a/an	the	some	any	many	a few
With uncountable nouns we use:			some	any	much	little

Example: We've had ......**some**...... terrible weather.

1 Let's go out for .... meal – I fancy .... pasta.
2 How .... garlic did you put in this spaghetti sauce?
3 In order to lose weight, I'm eating very .... fat.
4 Do you have .... idea how to prepare sashimi?
5 Have you got .... bowls? Yes, there are .... over here.
6 The café was busy and we had to wait .... minutes for .... table.
7 I don't think prawns need very .... cooking.
8 My friend Jenny is .... incredibly good cook.

Even though

Even though introduces a surprising or unexpected fact. It is stronger than *although* because of the adverb *even*.

Note that you can never use *even* on its own in this way:
~~Even I love sweet things, I never eat chocolate.~~
You must use *though* as well:
Even though I love sweet things, I never eat chocolate.
Even though I went to bed early last night, I am very tired today.

If you want to stress the fact that you are tired, you can reverse the order of the sentence:
I am very tired today, **even though** I went to bed early last night.

2 Scan the texts on page 15 of your Student's Book to find an example of *even though*. What is the surprising fact it introduces?

3 Complete each sentence with an appropriate subordinate clause.

1 Even though ....
   I failed the driving test.
2 Even though ....
   there were no seats left.
3 I was determined to enjoy the party, even though ....
   ....
4 The film was a success, even though ....
   ....
5 Even though ....
   there are too many cars on the roads.

Writing a recipe

1 Complete the recipe below using some of the verbs from the box. You will
not need all the verbs.

slice   stir   grill   sprinkle   heat   chop   mix   simmer   add   melt peel   beat   boil   spread   burn   grate   mash   fry   shake   bake

Shepherd's Pie

First, use a knife to peel and (1) .... an onion
and some garlic. (2) .... these in oil in a large
pan. Then, (3) .... some minced lamb,
tomatoes and diced carrots. Lower the heat and
(4) .... the ingredients for an hour.
Meanwhile, (5) .... and slice some potatoes.
(6) .... them in water for 20 minutes. Next,
use a fork to (7) .... the potatoes with butter.
Transfer the meat and vegetables to an oven-proof
dish and spread the potato mixture over it. After
that, gently (8) .... some grated cheese over
the potato. Finally, put the pie in the oven and
(9) .... it for half an hour.
Enjoy your meal!

2 Name two of your favourite dishes.

traditional name of dish	English translation (if there is one)	ingredients

3 Write a description of how to make one of your favourite dishes for an
English-speaking friend who would like the recipe.

Use some simple connecting words from the box to link your ideas (as in
the recipe above).

first   then   next   meanwhile   after that   finally

WORD LIST

accurate *adj* (p 20) correct or exact

analyse *v* (p 19) to examine the details of something carefully, in order to understand or explain it

benefit *n* (p 21) something that helps you or gives you an advantage

budget *n* (p 19) a plan that shows how much money you have and how you will spend it

category *n* (p 17) a group of people or things of a similar type

characteristic *n* (p 19) a typical or obvious quality that makes one person or thing different from others

commercial *adj* (p 15) intended to make a profit: *commercial television*

consumer *n* (p 19) someone who buys or uses goods or services

disease *n* (p 19) an illness caused by an infection or by a failure of health and not by an accident

enable *v* (p 14) to make someone able to do something, or to make something possible

extent *n* (p 20) area or length; amount: *to a certain extent* = partly

familiar *adj* (p 16) easy to recognize because of being seen, met, heard, etc. before

indicate *v* (p 21) to show that something exists or is likely to be true: *Recent evidence indicates that the skeleton is about three million years old.*

instead *adv* (p 18) in the place of someone or something else: *If you don't want pizza, we can have pasta instead.*

juice *n* (p 15) the liquid that comes from fruit or vegetables

level *n* (p 19) the amount or number of something: *The level of iron in her blood was too low.*

link *v* (p 20) to make a connection between two or more people, things, or ideas

market *n* (p 19) the buying and selling of something: *the insurance/personal computer market*

method *n* (p 19) a way of doing something, often one that involves a system or plan

mixture *n* (p 15) a substance made of other substances that have been combined: *Add milk to the mixture and stir until smooth.*

nowadays *adv* (p 19) at the present time, especially when compared to the past

originate *v* (p 20) to come from a particular place or person, or to begin during a particular period

outer *adj* (p 15) on the edge or surface of something: *Remove the outer layers of the onion.*

per *prep* (p 19) for each

popular *adj* (p 21) liked by many people

production *n* (p 20) when you make or grow something

purpose *n* (p 20) why you do something or why something exists: *The main purpose of the meeting is to discuss the future of the company.*

quality *n* (p 16) part of the character or personality of someone or something: *Joe has a lot of good qualities, but I don't think he has the ability to discipline the team.*

rate *v* (p 20) to judge the quality or ability of someone or something

recently *adv* (p 18) not long ago

regularly *adv* (p 20) often

researcher *n* (p 20) somebody who studies a subject in detail in order to discover new information about it

risk *n* (p 19) the possibility of something bad happening: *the risk of heart disease*

sense *n* (p 20) one of the five natural abilities of sight, hearing, touch, smell, and taste

similar *adj* (p 21) Something which is similar to something else has many things the same, although it is not exactly the same.

situation *n* (p 18) the set of things that are happening and the conditions that exist at a particular time and place

standard *n* (20) a pattern or model that is generally accepted: *This program is an industry standard for computers.*

throughout *adv, prep* (p 15) in every part of a place

update *v* (p 20) to make something more modern by adding new information or changing its design

variety *n* (p 21) a lot of different activities, situations, people, etc.

3 On the road

Compound nouns

In English we can combine two or three nouns to make a compound noun. This is a very neat way of saying something complex. The first noun acts as a modifier for the second, e.g. *air traffic* = **traffic** in the **air**, as opposed to road traffic, or *lost luggage claim form* = a **form** on which you can make a **claim** about **luggage** which has been **lost**.

1 Combine a word from box A with a word from box B to make up eleven compound nouns to do with travel. Use the word from box A first.

A
> air   business   credit   flight   insurance   tour
> package   arrivals   name   travel   hand

B
> attendant   trip   tag   card   luggage   hall
> insurance   tour   traffic   policy   guide

2 Complete each sentence with a compound noun from exercise 1.

Example: We waited for an hour in the ___arrivals hall___ for our bags.

1 He couldn't identify his luggage because the .... had fallen off.
2 It's essential to take out .... before you go on holiday.
3 We managed to book a really cheap .... to Thailand through our travel agent.
4 I'm going on a .... next week to Hong Kong to meet our agents and set up a new office there.
5 The .... was very helpful on the plane when I felt unwell.
6 You can get cash on your .... , so you don't need to take travellers' cheques overseas.

4 Make two compound nouns from each of the groups of words below.

Example: travel / holder / document   ___travel document, document holder___

1 text / mark / book   ....
2 guide / dog / tour   ....
3 school / language / bus   ....
4 holiday / adventure / destination   ....
5 hall / lecture / university   ....

Explain what all the compound nouns mean.

Articles

1 **Complete the paragraph below by putting a definite article (*the*), an indefinite article (*a/an*) or no article (–) in each space.**

RIVERS OF THE WORLD

The Mekong River, (1) .... tenth largest river in (2) .... world, has it origins in Tibet. (3) .... first two thousand kilometres of (4) .... river is in Chinese territory. It then flows 2,400 km through Myanmar, Laos, Thailand and Cambodia before entering (5) .... South China Sea through (6) .... huge delta in southern Vietnam sometimes called 'the nine-tailed dragon'. This area is known as (7) .... Lower Mekong Basin. Hardly anywhere in (8) .... world do more people depend on (9) .... single river than in this region. Fifty million people live here and more than 80% of these are directly dependent on (10) .... river through (11) .... fisheries and (12) .... agriculture.

The passive

2 **Look at the pictures and complete the speech bubbles using the passive form *was/were* + past participle.**

Example:

How did you break your leg?

I was knocked over by a car.

1 How did you lose your wallet?

It ....

2 Is that a famous painting?

Yes, it .... by Monet.

3 When did you get that little dog?

He .... to me for my birthday.

4 How old do you think these buildings are?

They .... 2000 years ago.

5 Where do you come from?

I .... in Poland, but I live in Canada.

6 Where does this rug come from?

It .... in Afghanistan.

Describing a journey using an itinerary

1 These words are from the reading passage about the Mekong on page 24 of the Student's Book. Can you explain them all? Use a dictionary to help you if necessary.

verbs (past simple)
docked / set off / headed off / head home / rushed / veered / disembark
nouns
traffic / driver / pedestrians / passengers / ferry
expressions of time or place
on board / once / in the morning / by mid morning / at first / at the last moment

2 Look at the map of Australia. Imagine that you and a friend have travelled from Cairns in the north to Melbourne in the south. You used several different means of transport and stopped along the way for sightseeing and recreation.

Using the table below, write a letter to another friend telling them about your journey. Imagine you are writing it on the plane going home. Use the past simple tense. Don't include more than two dates in your letter.

Cairns

Brisbane

Sydney

Melbourne

ITINERARY					
date	from	to	means of transport	things to do	accommodation
Mon 1 April	Cairns	Brisbane	bus – 2 days non-stop!	visit art gallery river trip to koala park	backpackers' hostel
Saturday	Brisbane	Sydney	air – 1hour	see Opera House harbour cruise beach / movies	with friends
Wed	Sydney	Blue mountains	train – 2 hours each way	walk in mountains visit waterfall	day trip only
Fri 12 April	Sydney	Melbourne	hire car – 4 days along coast road	see countryside beaches fishing	camping
Thur 18 April	Melbourne	home	air	shopping in melbourne	

3 Complete the table below for a journey you have been on. Then write an account of this journey.

date	from	to	means of transport	memories

WORDLIST

accurately *adv* (p 27) correctly or exactly

advice *n* (p 24) suggestions about what you think someone should do or how they should do something

agree *v* (p 22) to have the same opinion as someone

avoid *v* (p 24) to stay away from a person, place, situation, etc: *Try to avoid the city centre.*

border *n* (p 24) the line that separates two countries or states

commerce *n* (p 24) the activities involved in buying and selling things

description *n* (p 22) something that tells you what someone or something is like: *I gave the police a description of the stolen jewellery.*

diagram *n* (p 26) a simple picture showing what something looks like or explaining how something works

dialogue *n* (p 27) a conversation between two or more people

direction *n* (p 23) the way that someone or something is going or facing

expression *n* (p 27) a phrase that has a special meaning

finally *adv* (p 25) after a long time or some difficulty

impression *n* (p 24) an idea, feeling, or opinion about something or someone

legitimate *adj* (p 24) allowed by law

leisurely *adj* (p 24) in a relaxed way without hurrying

message *n* (p 26) a piece of written or spoken information which one person gives to another

minute *n* (p 23) a period of time equal to 60 seconds

mobile *n* (p 23) a mobile phone

object *n* (p 22) a thing that you can see or touch but that is usually not alive: *a bright, shiny object*

passenger *n* (p 23) someone who is travelling in a vehicle, but not controlling the vehicle

pedestrian *n* (p 24) a person who is walking and not travelling in a vehicle

pinpoint *v* (p 25) to say exactly what or where something is

produce *n* (p 24) food that is grown or made in large quantities to be sold

property *n* (p 23) objects that belong to someone

provide *v* (p 26) to supply something to someone: *This booklet provides useful information about local services.*

relieved *adj* (p 24) feeling happy because something unpleasant did not happen or you are not worried about something any more

religion *n* (p 24) the belief in a god or gods, or a particular system of belief in a god or gods

remaining *adj* (p 25) continuing to exist when everything or everyone else has gone or been dealt with

secondary *adj* (p 24) relating to the education of students aged between 11 and 18

sign *n* (p 24) something showing that something else exists or might happen or exist in the future: *I've searched for my hat, but there's no sign of it anywhere* (= I can't find it)

specific *adj* (p 26) exact or containing details

spectacular *adj* (p 24) extremely good, exciting, or surprising

steep *adj* (p 24) A steep slope, hill, etc. goes up or down very quickly.

summary *n* (p 25) a short description that gives the main facts or ideas about something

summit *n* (p 24) the top of a mountain

traditional *adj* (p 24) following the customs or ways of behaving that have continued in a group of people or society for a long time: *traditional Hungarian dress*

understand *v* (p 22) to know why or how something happens or works

uniform *n* (p 24) a special set of clothes that are worn by people who do a particular job or people who go to a particular school

useful *adj* (p 22) helping you to do or achieve something

view *n* (p 24) the things that you can see from a place: *There was a lovely view of the lake from the bedroom window.*

weekly *adj, adv* (p 27) happening once a week or every week

Enjoy, enjoyable, enjoyment

> The verb *enjoy* needs to be followed by an object (e.g. *I enjoyed the film*) or by a reflexive pronoun (*myself* / *yourself* / *himself* etc.).
>
> You can also use the adjective *enjoyable* and the noun *enjoyment*.

1 Use an appropriate form of the word *enjoy* to complete the sentences below. Use a reflexive pronoun if necessary.

1 We went out last night and we thoroughly ....
2 I don't find wrestling a very .... sport to watch.
3 Young children get a lot of .... from playing video games.
4 Did you .... your meal at the new restaurant last night?
5 People used to find the old black and white movies very ....
6 .... at the party tonight!

Compound adjectives

> Compound adjectives made up of a number and a noun are a convenient way to describe something which involves a number. You met an example of this on Student's Book page 30: 'The lighthouse at Genoa ... was rebuilt as a *two-section* brick tower.'
>
> When you form adjectives in this way:
> ▶ you do not include an *-s* on the word being counted: a **three-storey** building
> ▶ it is usual to add a hyphen: a **two-tier** education system.

2 Rewrite the following sentences so that the number comes before the noun being counted. You may need to supply this noun from the meaning, as shown in the example.

Example: It takes **four days** to travel from New York to Los Angeles by car.
It's a **four-day journey** by car from New York to Los Angeles.

1 My house has three bedrooms.
I live in ....
2 The insurance lasts for a period of 36 weeks.
The insurance covers ....
3 The flight from Bangkok to Sydney takes nine hours.
It's ....
4 Prices have gone up by 25 per cent.
There has been ....
5 The prize-winner was an artist who was 22 years old.
The prize-winner was ....

GRAMMAR

Comparatives and superlatives

1 **Complete the sentences by adding the correct comparative or superlative form of the adjective in brackets. You may need to include the words *the* or *than*.**

Example: My suitcase is ....*lighter than*.... yours. (light)

1 The winning team isn't always .... team. (good)

2 In some ways I prefer watching football on TV to going to the match because it's .... to see the players, but it's definitely ....(easy) (exciting)

3 Even though it's .... to cook at home, I prefer it to eating in restaurants. (time-consuming)

4 This is .... curry I have ever eaten. (hot)

5 My cold just got .... and .... until I finally went to the doctor. (bad)

6 Since I took the new job, I've got .... time than I had before. (little)

7 .... proportion of recently arrived migrants to Australia have settled in Sydney. (large)

8 This is .... novel I have ever read and I doubt whether I will manage to finish it. (interesting)

9 Of the three of us, my .... sister is by far .... (old) (tall)

10 That was .... film I have ever seen and I've seen some bad ones! (bad)

While, whereas, on the other hand

2 **Complete the passage using *while*, *whereas* or *on the other hand*.**

Many people like to take their holidays on or by the water, by hiring a houseboat and travelling along the rivers at a leisurely pace. (1) .... , if you want a bit more luxury, why not take a cruise? (2) .... we often associate the word 'cruise' with the idea of a floating hotel on the Caribbean Sea, cruises aren't always like this and there are many other options. Some people choose a small cruise ship, (3) .... others may prefer a romantic old paddle steamer such as *The Delta Queen*, a 77-year-old steamer, which cruises up and down the Mississippi river in America.

Comparing and contrasting data

1 Look at the two pie charts below.

1 What do the two charts have in common?
2 What is the essential difference between the two charts?

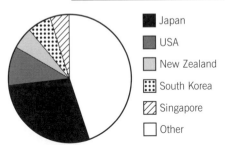

1991 Australian trade with the world

■ Japan
■ USA
□ New Zealand
▦ South Korea
▨ Singapore
□ Other

EXPORTS (coal, wheat, meat, textile fibres, manufactured goods)

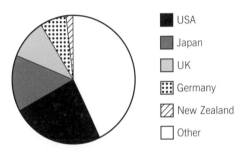

■ USA
■ Japan
□ UK
▦ Germany
▨ New Zealand
□ Other

IMPORTS (machinery, transport equipment, petroleum, manufactured goods)

2 Complete the paragraphs using information from the pie charts.

In 1991 Australia's main exports were raw materials, such as
(1) .... and (2) .... , whereas the main
(3) .... were machinery, petroleum and manufactured
goods.

Australia had five significant export markets in 1991, which together
accepted over (4) .... of the total goods sold. Of these, the
largest was (5) .... , which took about 25 per cent of
Australia's exports.

The largest single exporter to Australia, on the other hand, was
(6) .... , from where Australia received approximately
(7) .... of its imports. Other important trading partners
were (8) .... and (9) .... , who together
supplied another 25 per cent of imports.

WORD LIST

ancient *adj* (p 29) from a long time ago

approximately *adv* (p 32) close to a particular number or time although not exactly that number or time

beneath *prep, adv* (p 29) under something, or in a lower position than something

century *n* (p 30) a period of 100 years, especially used in giving dates

civilisation *n* (p 30) human society with its developed social organizations, or the culture and way of life of a society at a particular period of time

connected *adj* (p 30) If two things are connected, they are joined together.

creature *n* (p 29) anything that lives but is not a plant

differ *v* (p 31) to be different

discovery *n* (p 31) when someone discovers something: *Scientists have made some important discoveries about genetics recently.*

economic *adj* (p 30) using little money

exception *n* (p 31) someone or something that is not included in a rule, group, or list

expect *v* (p 29) to think that something will happen

famous *adj* (p 30) known or recognized by many people

global *adj* (p 30) relating to the whole world

graph *n* (p 33) a picture with measurements marked on it as lines or curves, used to compare different things or show the development of something

graphic *adj* (p 33) in the form of charts, diagrams, graphs, etc.

history *n* (p 30) the whole series of events in the past which relate to the development of a country, subject, or person

immense *adj* (p 29) extremely big

increase *v* (p 29) to get bigger or to make something bigger in size or amount

lecturer *n* (p 33) someone who teaches at a university or college

literally *adv* (p 30) having the real or original meaning of a word or phrase: *They were responsible for literally millions of deaths.*

meaning *n* (p 30) The meaning of words, signs, or actions is what they express or represent. *The word 'squash' has several meanings.*

modern *adj* (p 30) relating to the present time and not to the past

navigate *v* (p 30) to successfully sail along an area of water

occupy *v* (p 30) to fill a place or period of time

opinion *n* (p 31) a thought or belief about something or someone: *What's your opinion about/on the matter?*

paraphrase *n* (p 30) when something that has been said or written is expressed in a different way, usually so that it is clearer

population *n* (p 31) the number of people living in a particular area

procedure *n* (p 29) way of doing something

proportion *n* (p 32) a part of a total number or amount

protect *v* (p 30) to keep someone or something safe from something dangerous or bad

reliable *adj* (p 30) able to be trusted or believed

remind *v* (p 30) to make someone remember something, or remember to do something

satellite *n* (p 31) a piece of equipment that is sent into space around the Earth to receive and send signals or to collect information

sentence *n* (p 30) a group of words, usually containing a verb, that expresses a complete idea

sight *n* (p 30) something which you see, especially something interesting: *the sights and sounds of the market*

spelling *n* (p 33) how a particular word is spelt

syllable *n* (p 31) a word or part of a word that has one vowel sound: *'But' has one syllable and 'apple' has two syllables.*

uncertain *adj* (p 30) not known, or not completely certain: *The museum faces an uncertain future.*

urban *adj* (p 32) belonging or relating to a town or city

yet *adv* (p 31) before now or before that time: *Have you read his book yet?*

5 Come rain or shine

Describing geographic features

1 Choose an adjective from the box to complete the sentences. There are
some adjectives that you will not need.

| dry | dusty | fertile | flat | infertile | inhospitable |
| mountainous | rocky | vast | wet | | |

Example: In winter, the mountains are very ...inhospitable.... and few people
can live there.

1 No ships could land on the island because the coast was too ....
2 Because of the low annual rainfall, the Arizona desert is
.... and infertile.
3 Farmers rotate crops to ensure that the land remains ....
4 Holland is a very .... country, which means that it
constantly runs the risk of flooding.
5 The so-called .... regions of Australia are pretty low
compared to Europe, Asia and America.
6 If you cut down all the trees, the land becomes .... and
can eventually turn into a desert.

Finding the right word

2 Look at the following piece of writing on the topic of geography. Using the
'suggestions for changes' as a guide, try to improve the writing by finding
a more specific word or phrase to replace the underlined words.

What is geography and why do we study it?

Geography is the study of the differences which exist on
the Earth's surface. It is the ¹study of space and place
and it allows us to understand and respond to changes that
are ²happening in our rapidly changing world.
Geography is, by its very nature, an interesting
³topic and we can study it in a variety of ways. We can
learn about geography by reading ⁴books, by writing, by
listening and ⁵by doing things.
The more ways we use, the better we learn. Geography is
a practical area and those who are able to travel overseas
will gain a ⁶good opportunity to study the world at first
hand.
⁷People who study geography make use of maps, graphs,
photographs, diagrams, surveys and fieldwork reports, all of
which are vital ⁸origins of information. They are able to
⁹talk about and debate current issues of world importance
and ¹⁰get attitudes and values as citizens of the world.

Suggestions for changes
1. Avoid repetition - use a different word.
2. Use the expression 'take place'.
3. Use a different word meaning 'something you study at school or university'.
4. Unnecessary word.
5. Use the term 'personal experience' and change the preposition to 'through'.
6. More accurate adjective needed.
7. Use one word.
8. Use another word meaning 'where things come from'.
9. More specific verb needed.
10. 'get' is too simple here.

Checking for punctuation

1 Correct the punctuation and use of capital letters where necessary in the following letter to a friend.

There are also ten other errors. <u>Underline</u> them and write the words correctly in the margin. The first one has been done for you.

Dear Rhea,

Well another year has passed I just can't <u>beleve</u> that it went so quickly a year ago I was studying for my exams and now Im woking really hard at the bank. What a shock

And how are you, I hope that you Mothers recovered from her Accident in the park and is feeling better now. I was so sorry to here about that its very easy to slip over when theirs a lot of ice. On the ground. Luckly it isn't snowing here at the moment. However, the whether forecast isn't good. For the next few weeks.

Im writing to tell you that I hope to visit you in February or March if you have some free time then. Ive saved up some money so I will be able to aford a flight. Because there are some good discounts in the spring. Let me know when I should come and I'll start my plans.

We're all doing fine here. Timmy is starting school soon and Sarah has got a new boyfrend I'm not liking him much.

Take care

your good friend

May

Example:
believe

Zero article

2 Complete the paragraph with *the* (the definite article) or – (no article).

The Pyramids

To __the__ people of ancient Egypt, (1) _____ life on earth was short. Death, however, was eternal so they built their tombs of (2) _____ stone and they took (3) _____ food, (4) _____ clothing, (5) _____ jewellery and other possessions with them when they died.

(6) _____ tombs of the kings were (7) _____ most impressive of all, and were called the Pyramids. (8) _____ purpose of these huge stone mountains was to protect (9) _____ burial chamber from (10) _____ weather as well as from (11) _____ thieves.

Describing tables

1 Look at the table and complete the notes below by writing the name of the country in the gaps.

country	tourism receipts as % of exports
Egypt	66.8%
Jamaica	54.9%
Kenya	42.8%
Morocco	29.5%
Mexico	19.9%
Thailand	19.1%
The Philippines	15.0%

Tourism as a percentage of exports

The table provides information about the importance of tourism as an export in a number of different countries.

Tourism represents 42.8% of the total export revenue for (1) ...., whereas only 15% of the export revenue for (2) .... comes from this source.

The proportion of export earnings resulting from tourism in (3) .... is very similar to that earned in (4) .... and constitutes just under 20% of total export revenue.

(5) .... earns well over half of its export revenue from tourism, which sets it aside from the other countries shown in this table. Only (6) .... falls within a similar range.

Describing trends

2 Read the table. Are the statements below accurate or not? If they are not, rewrite them to reflect the information in the table accurately.

Tourist destinations – Number of tourists by region – (figures are in millions)

	Africa	Americas	East Asia Pacific	Europe	Middle East	South Asia
1960	0.8	15.2	–	45.8	–	–
1970	2.0	26.6	–	102.0	–	0.2
1980	6.9	46.8	18.4	195.0	–	0.9
1990	12.5	72	44.3	273.6	6.1	2.3
2000	17.0	84.0	86.2	338.2	6.8	3.4

1 Africa has been growing in popularity as a tourist destination over the last 40 years.
2 East Asia and the Pacific region have been popular destinations since the 1960s.
3 Tourism in the Middle East began in the 1980s and is growing rapidly.
4 Europe has seen a gentle increase in tourism since the 1960s.
5 There has been almost no increase in tourism in South Asia over the last ten years.

absolutely *adv* (p 35) used as a way of strongly saying 'yes'

actual *adj* (p 37) real, not guessed or imagined

against *prep* (p 34) protecting you from something bad: *Fresh fruit in the diet may protect against cancer.*

alternatively *adv* (p 37) used to give a second possibility

average *adj* (p 36) An average amount is calculated by adding some amounts together and then dividing by the number of amounts: *an average age/temperature*

clear *adj* (p 37) easy to understand

climate *n* (p 36) the weather conditions that an area usually has

concern *n* (p 38) a feeling of worry about something, or the thing that is worrying you

damage *n* (p 38) harm or injury

drought *n* (p 38) a long period when there is no rain and people do not have enough water

exaggerate *v* (p 35) to make something seem larger, better, worse, etc. than it really is

experience *n* (p 38) something that happens to you that affects how you feel

hesitate *v* (p 38) to pause before doing something, especially because you are nervous or not certain

illustrate *v* (p 36) to give more information or examples to explain or prove something to illustrate a point/problem

imagination *n* (p 38) the ability to create ideas or pictures in your mind

inadequate *adj* (p 39) not good enough or too low in quality

insurance *n* (p 38) an agreement in which you pay a company money and they pay your costs if you have an accident, injury, etc.

introduce *v* (p 37) to be the beginning of something; to speak or write before the beginning of a programme or book and give information about its contents

limit *n* (p 39) the largest amount of something that is possible or allowed

manager *n* (p 39) someone in control of an office, shop, team, etc.

maximum *adj* (p 36) The maximum amount of something is the largest amount that is allowed or possible.

necessary *adj* (p 36) needed in order to achieve something

news *n* (p 38) new information

occasion *n* (p 35) a time when something happens: *a previous/separate occasion*

official *n* (p 39) someone who has an important position in an organization such as the government

opportunity *n* (p 38) a situation in which it is possible for you to do something, or a possibility of doing something: *Don't miss this opportunity to win a million pounds.*

organisation *n* (p 38) the way that parts of something are arranged

overcome *v* (p 39) to deal with and control a problem or feeling

personally *adv* (p 35) used when you are going to give your opinion: *Personally, I'd rather stay at home and watch TV.*

problem *n* (p 39) a situation that causes difficulties and that needs to be dealt with

rewrite *v* (p 36) to write something again, often in order to improve it

repair *v* (p 38) to fix something that is broken or damaged

serious *adj* (p 38) A serious problem or situation is bad and makes people worry. *a serious accident/illness*

statement *n* (p 36) something that someone says or writes

system *n* (p 39) a set of connected pieces of equipment that operate together: *They've had an alarm system installed at their home.*

terribly *adv* (p 35) very badly

trend *n* (p 36) a general development or change in a situation

weak *adj* (p 35) difficult to see or hear: *He spoke in a weak voice.*

wrong *adj* (p 39) If something is wrong, there is a problem.

UNIT 6 Value for money

VOCABULARY

Money words

1 Complete the conversations using words from the box.

Example: A We have a lot of cut-price items on ....sale......... today. Can I interest you in anything?
B I'm afraid these ....prices......... are still too high for me.

1 A If I .... enough money this year, I'm going to have a holiday in February.
B That's a good idea. You can get some .... at that time of year.

2 A I see you've finished your meal. Would you like the .... now, sir?
B OK. Is there a .... for service?

3 A How much does a theatre ticket .... for tonight's show?
B 30$, but if you're under 18, you get a $5 ....

4 A I want to have horse-riding lessons but I can't .... them.
B Never mind. Looking after a horse can be very ....

> ~~prices~~
> save
> charge
> cost
> bargains
> bill
> discount
> afford
> ~~sale~~
> expensive

Word meaning

2 Here is an extract from the *Cambridge Advanced Learner's Dictionary* that shows part of the entry for the word *value* and other words related to it.

> **value** /'væl.juː/ *verb* [T] to consider something important: *I've always valued her advice.*
> **valued** /'væl.juːd/ *adj FORMAL* useful and important: *a valued member of staff*
> **values** /'væl.juːz/ *plural noun* the beliefs people have about what is right and wrong and what is most important in life, which control their behaviour: *family/moral/traditional values*
> **value** MONEY /'væl.juː/ *noun* [C or U] the amount of money which can be received for something: *She had already sold everything of value that she possessed.* ○ *What is the value of the prize?* ○ *The value of the pound fell against other European currencies yesterday.* ○ *Property values have fallen since the plans for the airport were published.* ○ *I thought the offer was good value (for money)/[US ALSO] a good value* (= a lot was offered for the amount of money paid).
> **valuable** /'væl.jʊ.bl̩/ *adj* worth a lot of money: *These antiques are both beautiful and extremely valuable.* ○ *This is losing valuable business for the company.* *NOTE: The opposite is worthless. Invaluable means 'extremely useful'.*
> **valuables** /'væl.jʊ.blz/ *plural noun* small objects, especially jewellery, which might be sold for a lot of money.

Complete the sentences by choosing an appropriate word or expression.

Example: Old people sometimes feel that young people don't ....value......... them or pay them enough respect.

1 Over the centuries, the .... of society have changed.
2 The most .... paintings in the gallery are next to the reception area.
3 Eating in this restaurant is always good ....
4 My penknife was .... on the camping trip and I couldn't have managed without it.
5 When I go away on holiday, I always lock up all my .... at home.

GRAMMAR

Using 'worth'

1 **Rewrite the following sentences using *worth* or an appropriate form of it. Use your dictionary to help you.**

Example: I need to change £500 into Japanese yen.

I need £500 worth of Japanese yen.

1 How much do you think you could sell your old car for?

....

2 It took a long time to get to the museum but I'm glad we went.

....

3 The diving certificate that I got on holiday doesn't seem to be recognised here.

....

4 Is that book on global warming any good?

....

5 You can't get much money for a second-hand computer.

....

Tenses and verb forms

2 **Complete the description of the graph below by using an appropriate verb in the correct tense or form.**

Extraordinary growth in Indian IT software and services industry, value in $bn

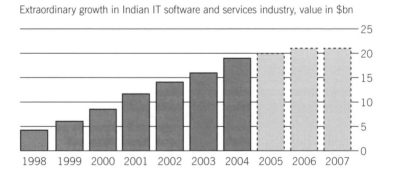

In 1998 the Indian software industry was worth just under 4 billion dollars. Between 1998 and 2000, this figure (1) .... to just over 8 billion dollars and since 2000 there (2) .... a dramatic increase in the value of this industry. The greatest rise (3) .... from 2000 to 2001 when it (4) .... by 4 billion dollars.

In the near future, the value of the industry (5) .... to grow more steadily and economists (6) .... that in the year 2006, the trend (7) .... at 21 billion dollars.

Introducing a graph

1 Write one sentence to say what each graph shows.

1 Down, but levelling off

Spain's unemployment rate,%

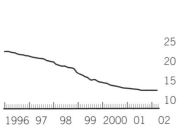

2 High-budget films

Production costs per film in America $m

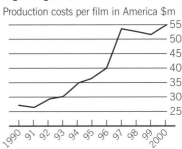

Describing the overall trends

2 Write one sentence that describes what each graph shows and a second sentence that describes the overall trends.

1 The cost of progress

China's net imports of oil, tonnes m

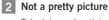

2 Not a pretty picture

Television-advertising market, $m

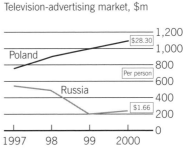

Selecting important details

3 Write a paragraph that describes what this graph shows and describes the overall trend. Write a second paragraph, selecting data from the graph that illustrate the trends. Then write a simple conclusion.

Cleaning up

Concentrations in London, micrograms per cubic metre

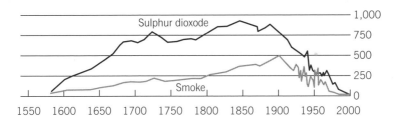

Unit 6 Value for money

accuracy *n* (p 45) how correct or exact something is

admire *v* (p 40) to respect or approve of someone or something

annual *adj* (p 42) measured over a period of one year

appear *v* (p 41) to start to be seen: *Then a bright light appeared in the sky.*

birthrate *n* (p 43) a measurement of the number of babies born in a particular period

central *adj* (p 40) controlled or organized in one main place

commodity *n* (p 40) a product that you can buy or sell

concern *v* (p 43) If a story, film, etc concerns a particular subject, it is about that subject.

concluding *adj* (p 44) last in a series of things

content *n* (p 40) the information or ideas that are talked about in a book, speech, film, etc.

continuous *adj* (p 40) happening or existing without stopping

cover *v* (p 44) to include or deal with a subject or piece of information: *The book covers European history from 1789–1914.*

decade *n* (p 43) a period of ten years

destination *n* (p 42) the place where someone or something is going

elsewhere *adv* (p 43) in or to another place

expert *n* (p 40) someone who has a lot of skill in something or a lot of knowledge about something

explain *v* (p 44) to make something clear or easy to understand by giving reasons for it or details about it

figure *n* (p 43) a number that expresses an amount, especially in official documents: *Government figures show a rise in unemployment.*

forecaster *n* (p 43) someone who says what is likely to happen in the future: *a weather forecaster*

gap *n* (p 40) an empty space or hole in the middle of something, or between two things

growth *n* (p 42) when something grows, increases, or develops

identify *v* (p 42) to recognize someone or something and say or prove who or what they are

invention *n* (p 40) something that has been designed or created for the first time

issue *v* (p 40) to produce or provide something official: *to issue a passport/ticket/ invitation*

mention *v* (p 44) to briefly speak or write about something or someone

present *n* (p 43) the period of time that is happening now

produce *v* (p 41) to make or grow something

realise *v* (p 40) to notice or understand something that you did not notice or understand before

recognise *v* (p 40) to know someone or something because you have seen or experienced them before: *I recognised her from her picture.*

salary *n* (p 40) a fixed amount of money that you receive from your employer, usually every month

software *n* (p 44) programs that you use to make a computer do different things

staff *n* (p 42) the people who work for an organization

supply *n* (p 40) an amount of something that is ready to be used: *a supply of water*

tour operator *n* (p 43) a company that arranges holidays for people

trade *v* (p 41) to buy and sell goods or services, especially between countries

trend *n* (p 42) a general development or change in a situation

vertical *adj* (p 44) pointing straight up from a surface

visitor *n* (p 43) someone who visits a person or place

UNIT 7 Ignorance is bliss

Complete the puzzle.

Across

2 American word for a mark in an exam (5)

4 what you write on (5)

8 another word for 'took' (an exam) (3)

10 adjective to describe someone who studies a lot (8)

11 what you pay for a course (3)

12 a writing tool (3)

13 opposite of 'optional' (10)

15 'I ....' is another way of saying 'I understand' (3)

16 a fellow student or equal (4)

17 Journalists .... the news. (6)

20 something you pay in advance (7)

21 a break in a programme of events (8)

22 what you take at the end of a course (4)

24 a building where you find a lot of books (7)

25 a type of chart with data (5)

28 one of the IELTS modules (8)

29 opposite of 'theoretical' (9)

30 Your IELTS result is a band .... (5)

Down

1 an item of furniture in a study (4)

2 a sport that you play using clubs (4)

3 Continuous .... can be used instead of an exam. (10)

4 Students may work on this together. (7)

5 opposite of 'fail' (4)

6 to put your name forward; to enrol (8)

7 opposite of 'even' (3)

9 another word for 'semester' (4)

13 past tense of verb meaning 'handle successfully' (5)

14 It can be measured: also an act. (11)

15 You may use a questionnaire to help you conduct a ....
of people's views. (6)

18 You must use .... ideas in your Task 2 essay. (8)

19 small group sessions with the tutor (9)

23 preposition (2)

26 past tense of 'lay' (4)

27 You may keep your lecture notes in this. (4)

29

Tenses

GRAMMAR

1 Complete the sentences below from a college magazine using the verb in brackets in an appropriate tense.

Example: Despite their efforts, some students (fail) ......*failed*...... to find suitable accommodation last year.

1 In a recent survey, most students stated that they (prefer) .... living in shared accommodation.

2 Two weeks ago the painters (finally finish) .... decorating the halls of residence.

3 The accommodation officer (accept) .... a new position and will be leaving next September.

4 The library (just receive) .... 30,000 new books.

5 Some students (not yet pay) .... their deposits for using IT equipment.

6 Seventy per cent of students (consult) .... the International Student Officer since the beginning of the year.

7 It is important to let the college know which exams you (take) .... before coming to this country.

8 Fee forms were returned to students who (not write) .... their reference number at the top.

2 Complete the responses to the questions using the words in brackets.

Example: How did you get to college this morning?
I ...*came by public transport*................. (come / public transport)

1 Are you good at time management?
No, ... good at time management. (never / be)

2 How long did it take you to write your History essay?
I .... it. (spend / two weeks)

3 What type of accommodation do you prefer?
I .... on my own, but now .... shared accommodation. (like / live) (prefer)

4 When did you apply to join the mountaineering club?
I'm afraid I .... yet. (apply)

5 Why didn't you get tickets for the new Brad Pitt film?
Because I thought you .... (already / see)

Checking for tense errors

Maria has just started a new course at college and her tutor has asked her to write him a letter telling him something about herself. She has made ten mistakes in verb tenses in her letter. Find and correct them.

Dear Tutor,

I have come

~~I am coming~~ to Saltfield College from Hong Kong, where I was a student for ten years. I did already take examinations in Hong Kong in English, Physics, Chemistry and Maths. My highest score is for Maths: I got grade A.

When I was a student in Hong Kong I also have a part-time job in a shop. My uncle owns a dry-cleaning company and so I helped him in the evenings. I used to worked there four nights a week and I think this was very good experience for me.

At the weekends, I usually played basketball with friends or, if the weather's bad, we have been to the cinema, which is very popular in Hong Kong. Because of my part-time job, I also did spend a lot of time studying at the weekend.

I didn't go to many other places. My father took me to Singapore once. Three weeks after we had returned he also went to China and took the whole family.

This is a brief description of my background.

Best wishes,

Maria

WORD LIST

appearance *n* (p 48) the way a person or thing looks

apply *v* (p 47) to ask officially for something, often by writing: *I've applied for a job/grant/visa.*

appreciate *v* (p 49) to understand how good something or someone is and be able to enjoy them

behaviour *n* (p 48) the way that someone does or says things

beneficial adj (p 49) helpful or useful

cheat *v* (p 53) to behave in a way that is not honest or fair in order to win something or to get something

culture *n* (p 53) way of life, especially the habits, traditions, and beliefs of a country, society, or group of people

degree *n* (p 47) a qualification given for completing a university course: *She has a degree in physics.*

dress *v* (p 53) to wear a particular type, style, or colour of clothes

encourage *v* (p 46) to talk or behave in a way that gives someone confidence to do something: *My parents encouraged me to try new things.*

enrol *v* (p 51) to become or make someone become an official member of a course, college, or group

environment *n* (p 48) the situation that you live or work in, and how it influences how you feel

evidence *n* (p 48) something that makes you believe that something is true or exists: *There is no scientific evidence that the drug is addictive.*

extracurricular adj (p 46) describes an activity or subject that is not part of the usual school or college course

fail *v* (p 51) not to do something which you should do: *He failed to arrive on time.*

fee *n* (p 51) an amount of money that you pay to do something, to use something, or to get a service: *university fees*

formal adj (p 53) used about clothes, language, and behaviour that are serious and not friendly or relaxed

grade *n* (p 53) a number or letter that shows how good someone's work or performance is: *Carla got a grade A in German.*

habit *n* (p 57) something that you do regularly, almost without thinking about it

handbook *n* (p 46) a book that contains information and advice about a particular subject

inappropriate adj (p 53) not suitable

indication *n* (p 53) a sign showing that something exists or is likely to be true

initiative *n* (p 53) *to take the initiative* means to do things without needing to be told what to do

international adj (p 51) relating to or involving two or more countries

opinion *n* (p 46) a thought or belief about something or someone

participation *n* (p 53) the involvement with other people in an activity

previous adj (p 47) existing or happening before something or someone else

quote *v* (p 53) to repeat what someone has said or written

refund *n* (p 51) an amount of money that is given back to you, especially because you are not happy with something you have bought

semester *n* (p 51) one of the two time periods that a school or college year is divided into

smart adj (p 52) If you look smart or your clothes are smart, you look clean, tidy and stylish.

solve *v* (p 46) to find the answer to something

specialist *n* (p 46) someone who has a lot of experience, knowledge, or skill in a particular subject

strict adj (p 48) If a rule, law, etc is strict, it must be obeyed. A strict person makes sure that children or people working for them behave well and does not allow them to break any rules.

theme *n* (p 46) the subject of a book, film, speech, etc.

timetable *n* (p 46) a list of dates and times that shows when things will happen

viewpoint *n* (p 49) a way of thinking about a situation

welfare *n* (p 46) Someone's welfare is their health and happiness.

workload *n* (p 46) the amount of work that you have to do

8 *Fit as a fiddle*

Describing pain and illness

1 Choose a suitable adjective or verb from the box to complete the sentences. You may need to change the form of the verb. Sometimes more than one answer is possible.

> *adjectives*: stiff broken sore painful swollen
> *verbs*:   hurt sting twist water scratch

Example: I hit my finger with a hammer and now it's very ....*swollen*.... .

1 I .... my ankle playing football on Saturday.
2 I can hardly talk because I've got a really .... throat.
3 Toothache can be extremely ....
4 I cut my finger while slicing some lemons and it really ....
5 I fell over at work and hurt my arm. It may well be ....
6 I can't turn my head because I have a .... neck.
7 Peeling onions makes my eyes ....
8 I fell off my bike and .... my face.

Finding a remedy

2 Choose a 'remedy' (A–I) from the box for each problem in exercise 1.

> *Why don't you ...*
> A ... take an aspirin?   E ... rub in some ointment?
> B ... try some eye drops?   F ... put a bandage on it?
> C ... use some disinfectant?   G ... go to the hospital casualty department?
> D ... rinse it with water?   H ... suck some lozenges?
>   I ... put an ice pack on it?

Example: I

1 .... 2 .... 3 .... 4 .... 5 .... 6 .... 7 .... 8 ....

Compound nouns

3 Combine a word from box A with a word from box B to make eight compound nouns which are related to health.

A

heart first-aid side emergency blood health
hospital ambulance

B
surgery driver effects care attack staff
course pressure

GRAMMAR

Conditionals

1 Complete the sentences with *will, won't, would* or *wouldn't*.

Example: I ...*won't*... keep you waiting, if I can help it.

1 I .... climb that ladder, if I were you. It looks dangerous.

2 The restaurant .... open again as soon as they can find a new chef.

3 If humans were less territorial, the world .... be a much more civilised place.

4 I .... definitely go and see the new Harry Potter film when it comes to our local cinema.

5 I .... be able to go to the party on Saturday, unless I finish all this homework.

2 Complete the first part of the sentences using the words in brackets. Add *if* where necessary.

Example: (ring bell) .....*If you ring the bell*..... someone will answer the door.

1 (speak more English) .... if I went to the USA.

2 (not post my letter today) .... it won't get there on time.

3 (win the lottery) .... I'd give away a lot of the money.

4 (people drive more slowly) .... there would be fewer accidents.

5 (not miss the plane) .... if we arrive at the airport on time.

3 Complete the sentences using the words in brackets.

1 If global warming continues, ... (Earth's temperature / rise)

2 If more people moved out of the cities, ... (pollution levels / fall)

3 If .... there would be less crime. (be / more police)

4 If .... , you will earn more money. (do / lot / overtime)

The verb 'can'

4 Complete the sentences with *can, can't, could* or *couldn't*.

Woman: (1) .... you use chopsticks?

Man: I (2) .... now, but I
(3) .... when I first tried.

Woman: OK, (4) .... you ask the waiter for some then?

Describing information in tables

1 Look at the table below and answer these questions.

1 What is the table about? (Give the topic and time frame.)
2 What is the purpose of the table?
3 Can you find any trends – upward or downward trends?
4 What can you compare using the data?
5 Why do you think there is a category referred to as 'other'?

Composition of industry in the region of Melaka in Malaysia

industry sector	1990 %	1995 %	2000 %
Agriculture	18.5	16.0	10.1
Manufacturing	24.5	33.4	40.2
Construction	3.6	3.2	3.1
Hotels – tourism	12.2	13.3	14.9
Government sector	17.7	13.3	10.1
Finance, insurance	10.8	10.5	10.7
Other	12.7	10.3	10.9
Total	100	100	100

2 Here is a sentence explaining what the table is about.

The table provides data on the changing size of different industries in the Melaka region of Malaysia, over the ten-year period from 1990 to 2000.

Now write sentences based on the data contained in the table.

1 Write a sentence comparing two significant pieces of information.

....

....

2 Write a sentence describing a downward trend.

....

....

3 Write a sentence describing an upward trend.

....

....

4 Write a sentence highlighting a stable feature.

....

....

5 Write a sentence summing up the information.

....

....

WORD LIST

adequate *adj* (p 59) enough

adult *n* (p 57) a person or animal that has finished growing and is not now a child

afford *v* (p 59) to have enough money to buy something or have enough time to do something

allow *v* (p 55) to give someone permission for something

authority *n* (p 60) an official group or government department with power to control particular public services

budget *n* (p 59) the amount of money you have for something

burden *n* (p 60) something difficult or unpleasant that you have to deal with or worry about

certainly *adv* (p 61) used to emphasize something and show that there is no doubt about it: *Their team certainly deserved to win.*

change *v* (p 56) to become different, or to make someone or something become different

charity *n* (p 60) an official organization that gives money, food, or help to people who need it

checklist *n* (p 60) a list of things that you should think about, or that you must do

clinic *n* (p 60) a place where people go for medical treatment or advice

condition *n* (p 60) *on condition that* = only if

confuse *v* (p 56) to think that one person or thing is another person or thing: *Students sometimes confuse these two verbs.*

dangerous *adj* (p 54) If someone or something is dangerous, they could harm you.

definitely *adv* (p 56) without any doubt

discomfort *n* (p 54) slight pain

drug *n* (p 60) a chemical substance used as a medicine

estimate *n* (p 60) a guess of what a size, value, amount, etc might be

excellent *adj* (p 59) very good, or of a very high quality

experiment *n* (p 60) a test, especially a scientific one, that you do in order to learn something or discover if something is true

fair *adj* (p 60) If something, such as a price or share, is fair, it is reasonable and is what you expect or deserve.

injury *n* (p 58) damage to someone's body in an accident or attack

keen *adj* (p 61) very interested or enthusiastic

local *adj* (p 59) relating to an area near you

meanwhile *adv* (p 60) in the time between two things happening, or while something else is happening

measure *v* (p 60) to find the size, weight, amount or speed of something

poverty *n* (p 59) when you are very poor

recover *v* (p 55) to become healthy or happy again after an illness, injury, or period of sadness

relation *n* (p 60) a connection between two or more things

relative *adj* (p 61) compared to other similar things or people

remain *v* (p 57) to continue to exist when everything or everyone else has gone

repeat *v* (p 61) to say or do something more than once

representative *adj* (p 60) typical of, or the same as, others in a larger group of people or things: *a representative sample/cross-section/selection*

request *n* (p 56) when you politely or officially ask for something

rural *adj* (p 60) relating to the countryside and not to towns

stable *adj* (p 57) not likely to change or end suddenly

steadily *adv* (p 57) happening at a gradual, regular rate

survey *n* (p 60) an examination of people's opinions or behaviour made by asking people questions

treatment *n* (p 60) something which you do to try to cure an illness or injury, especially something suggested or done by a doctor

unavailable *adj* (p 59) impossible to buy or get

unconscious *adj* (p 58) in a state as though you are sleeping, for example because you have been hit on the head

victim *n* (p 58) someone who has suffered the effects of violence, illness, or bad luck

wealthy *adj* (p 61) rich

UNIT 9 *The driving force*

VOCABULARY

Describing cars

1 **Put the adjectives from the box in the correct part of the table according to which features of a car they describe.**

> medium-sized ~~cheap~~ economical executive ~~expensive~~ fast
> high-performance large luxury ~~reasonably priced~~ reliable safe
> smart spacious thirsty uneconomical

cost	expensive, cheap, reasonably priced
safety	
image	
performance	
fuel consumption	
size	

Compound nouns

2 **Combine a word from box A with a word from box B to form compound nouns.**
Use the compound nouns to complete the sentences below.

Example: It's quicker to use _public transport_ when the roads are very congested.

A	B
driving	belt
fuel	hour
~~public~~	jams
rush	licence
seat	lights
speed	limit
steering	tank
traffic	~~transport~~
traffic	wheel

1 The driver gripped the .... as he accelerated past the line of heavy trucks.
2 I avoid driving during the .... when there are lots of cars on the road.
3 It is illegal to travel in a car without wearing a ....
4 When you get to the .... , go straight ahead and the post office is on your right.
5 In Britain, the .... on the motorways is 70 miles per hour.
6 The increased use of cars for short journeys is causing .... in many cities.
7 When the police stopped the car, they found that the driver did not have a current ....
8 The .... in my new car holds 60 litres.

37

Because and because of

1 Rewrite the second part of sentences 1–8, using *because of* and the word in brackets.

Example: We got lost on the journey to Portsmouth because I'm not good
at reading maps. (skills)
... *because of my poor map-reading skills.*

1 We decided not to eat our lunch outdoors because it was a very hot day. (weather)
2 The medicine has been withdrawn from the market because it gives people headaches. (side-effects)
3 The document had to be rewritten because some of the facts in it were incorrect. (errors)
4 The boy goes to a special school because he can't hear well. (deafness)
5 You shouldn't eat chocolate because it is fattening. (fat content)
6 I would never go scuba diving because it is dangerous. (dangers)
7 I gave up smoking because I got ill. (health)
8 The children aren't allowed to watch TV because they have behaved so badly. (behaviour)

Linking words

2 Complete each sentence using a linking word or expression from the box. Try to use as many different expressions as you can.

however	because	because of	but	since	as
even though	also	so			

Example: I didn't enjoy the theatre performance ...*because*... my seat was
too far from the stage.

1 There's a 50-kilometre speed limit on this coast road .... most drivers go faster than that.
2 .... 'Shrek' is a children's film, parents like watching it too.
3 .... there had been no customers all day, the manager decided to close the shop early.
4 My husband always gets up at 6.30 am .... I tend to get up at the same time.
5 Gemma likes this restaurant .... the friendly atmosphere.
6 Studying all night before an exam is foolish .... you feel so tired the next day.
7 .... you like eating so much, why don't you cook tonight?
8 I like sports cars. .... , I don't want to buy one for myself.
9 I've done the washing up and I've .... cleaned the kitchen.
10 Mario speaks very little Spanish .... his mother is from Chile.

Collective nouns

When you describe a diagram, it is often useful to use a collective term.
This is a noun or compound noun that groups together related words,
e.g. *features*.

1 Match the groups of words on the left with the collective terms in the box.

Example: red, blue, silver   *colours*

1 tennis courts, pools, showers, sauna
2 cars, trucks, motorbikes
3 steering, reversing, parking
4 friendly, helpful, critical
5 country, city, suburbs

vehicles
skills
~~colours~~
areas
facilities
attitudes

Describing a table

2 Complete the description of the table using an appropriate word, words or number.

reasons for shopping at BJs supermarket	no. of men	no. of women
close to home	23	18
good reputation	15	20
24-hour shopping	2	0
parking facilities	19	18
friendly staff	4	4
competitive prices	12	15

The table shows the main reasons why BJs is a popular ....*supermarket*.... for
shoppers. The top three reasons are its (1).., its
reputation and its parking facilities. Of these, the most important reason why
men shop at BJs is that the shop is close to their home – (2)................................
men rated this as an important factor. (3)................................,
however, prefer BJs to other supermarkets mainly because
(4).. . They rated the location of the
supermarket second. A significant number of both men and women also choose
to shop at BJs because (5)................................ good parking facilities.
The women (6)................................ this was as important as the location
of the supermarket. On the other hand, the attitude of the staff does not seem to
be an important factor (7)................................ only four women and four
men rated this highly. Surprisingly, almost no one said they prefer
(8)................................ at BJs because it is open 24 hours a day.

WORD LIST

advertising *n* (p 65) the business of trying to persuade people to buy products or services

alternative *n* (p 65) one of two or more things that you can choose between

awareness *n* (p 66) the state of knowing about something

combine *v* (p 64) to become mixed or joined, or to mix or join things together: *The band combines jazz rhythms and romantic lyrics.*

commercial *n* (p 65) an advertisement on the radio or television

congestion *n* (p 65) when something is full or blocked, especially with traffic

contradict *v* (p 66) If two things that are said or written about something contradict each other, they are so different that they cannot both be true: *His account of the accident contradicts the official government report.*

controversial *adj* (p 65) causing a lot of disagreement or argument

convenience *n* (p 65) when something is easy to use and suitable for what you want to do: *the convenience of credit cards*

create *v* (p 65) to make something happen or exist

current *adj* (p 65) happening or existing now

demand *n* (p 65) a need for something to be sold or supplied: *There's an increasing demand for cheap housing.*

emission *n* (p 65) when gas, heat, light, etc. is sent out into the air, or an amount of gas, heat, light, etc. that is sent out

estimate *v* (p 65) to guess the cost, size, value, etc. of something

false *adj* (p 66) not true or correct

feature *n* (p 63) a typical quality, or important part of something: *This phone has several new features.*

greenhouse gas n (p 65) a gas which causes the greenhouse effect, i.e. an increase in the amount of carbon dioxide and other gases in the atmosphere which is believed to be the cause of a gradual warming of the surface of the Earth

highlight *v* (p 64) to emphasize something or make people notice something: *to highlight a problem/danger*

illustrate *v* (p 64) to give more information or examples to explain or prove something

impact *n* (p 65) the effect that a person, event, or situation has on someone or something

industry *n* (p 65) people and activities involved in one type of business: *the computer industry; manufacturing industries*

journey *n* (p 65) when you travel from one place to another

lifestyle *n* (p 65) the way that you live

option *n* (p 65) a choice

output *n* (p 65) the amount of something that is produced

pollution *n* (p 65) damage caused to water, air, etc by harmful substances or waste

pressure *n* (p 65) when someone tries to make someone else do something by arguing, persuading, etc: *Teachers are under increasing pressure to work longer hours.*

priority *n* (p 65) something that is very important and that must be dealt with before other things

rapid *adj* (p 65) happening or moving very quickly

regulation *n* (p 62) an official rule that controls how something is done

scheme *n* (p 65) an official plan or system

significance *n* (p 64) the importance or meaning of something

solution *n* (p 65) the answer to a problem

status *n* (p 65) the position that you have in relation to other people because of your job or social position

sustainable *adj* (p 65) causing little or no damage to the environment and therefore able to continue for a long time

vegetarian *n* (p 62) someone who does not eat meat or fish

vital *adj* (p 65) necessary

wildlife *n* (p 65) animals, birds, and plants living in their natural environment

10 *The silver screen*

Film words

1 The words and phrases below are used when talking about books. Think of an equivalent word or phrase that is used with films. (Check the extract on page 70 of your Student's Book.) Some words can be used for both films and books.

Example: page   screen

1 readers	6 book launch ....
2 plot	7 book critic ....
3 chapters	8 editor ....
4 characters	9 publishing world ....
5 main character	

2 These adjectives can describe a film or storyline. Match each adjective with an adjective in the box that expresses the same meaning but more strongly.

Example: funny hilarious		5 sad	....
1 bad	....	6 dull	....
2 interesting	....	7 violent	....
3 exciting	....	8 hopeful	....
4 frightening	....	9 unrealistic	....

boring	brutal	far-fetched	fascinating°	gripping
hilarious°	optimistic	terrible°	terrifying°	tragic

*You cannot use *very* with the asterisked words because their meaning is too strong.

3 Complete the review using words from the box.

costumes	special effects	stunts	dialogue
box office	soundtrack		

The film *Harry Potter and the Philosopher's Stone* is based on the first of the books by J.K. Rowling. It is an excellent attempt at re-creating the magic of the books. The (1) .... is just like the original, with the actors often using the exact words as they were written. The characters all look very realistic and they are dressed in the sort of (2) .... you imagine when you read the book. Only the (3) .... is truly original because, of course, there isn't any music in the book.

The scene where the children are learning to ride their broomsticks has some amazing (4) .... which create a wonderful magical atmosphere. It also required a number of clever (5) .... which must have been quite dangerous. When the film was released, it had record ticket sales at the (6) ....

GRAMMAR

Tense revision

1 **Choose the present perfect or past simple tense to complete each sentence correctly.**

Example: I lived / ~~have lived~~ in Hong Kong all my life.

1 My sister *has joined / joined* the local film club three years ago.
2 River levels *have been / were* high since the typhoon last month.
3 The number of students in the Arts faculty *has risen / rose* steadily last year.
4 *Haven't we seen / Didn't we see* this play when we were on holiday in Canada?
5 The government still *hasn't improved / didn't improve* public transport.
6 That was one of the best games of tennis I *have ever played / ever played*.
7 The physics lecture was more interesting than I *have expected / expected*.

2 **Complete each sentence with a verb in the present perfect continuous tense.**

Example: I ..*have been travelling*.. (travel) for the past three days.

1 Why .... (Jenny / learn) Japanese? Is she planning to visit the country?
2 What .... (you / do) since you arrived in Sydney last week?
3 My father .... (work) in the retail industry for a long time.
4 I .... (dream) about this football match all night long.
5 Sorry I'm late. I .... (help) my brother with his homework.
6 Maggie .... (try) to decide which science project to undertake.
7 How are you? .... (you / feel) any better since you went to see the doctor?

3 **Complete the sentences by putting the verbs in brackets into the correct tense. Make any other necessary changes.**

Example: I (born) ...*was born*... in Hong Kong but now I live in Vancouver.

1 My brother (learn) .... English for the past ten years so he speaks it well.
2 (you / always / be) .... good at singing?
3 I feel rather tired today because I (study) .... hard all week – I also (stay up) .... late last night.
4 How long ago (your sister / divorce) ....?
5 Since we (move) .... to Melbourne, my father (be unable) .... to find a job.
6 I'm very excited about the fact that my parents (decide) .... to buy a new apartment.
7 I (know) .... Jamie since we (enrol) .... on the same computer course.

WRITING

Autiobiography

1 **Write a short paragraph about yourself. Use these questions to help you:**

- Where were you born?
- What school did you go to?
- Are you married? (When and where did you get married?)
- When did you start studying English?
- How long have you been studying English?
- How many English exams have you passed?

When you have finished, underline all your verbs and make sure the tenses are correct.

Biography

2 **Using the details below, write a short biographical article about Jackie Chan.**

Paragraph 1 Jackie's family background, childhood and education
Paragraph 2 How Jackie's career developed
Paragraph 3 Other interesting facts about Jackie, including his most recent achievement

Jackie Chan BIOGRAPHY

Personal details

Nationality:	Chinese
Place of birth:	Hong Kong
Date of birth:	1954
Father's occupation:	cook
Mother's occupation:	housekeeper
Type of actor:	comedy stuntman
Injuries:	nearly every bone broken including skull fracture

Film career

Age 7–17: Peking Opera School (acrobatics, martial arts, etc.)

Age 8: First film: *Big and Little Wong Tin Bar* (drama)

1971: First leading role: *Master with Cracked Fingers* (Hong Kong)

First successful film across Asia: *Drunken Master* (comedy adventure)

1995: *Rumble in the Bronx* was No. 1 at US box office

1995: Lifetime Achievement Award from US cable network MTV

MTV award: Best fight scene in *Rush Hour* (1998)

WORD LIST

Unit 10 *The silver screen*

achieve v (p 70) to succeed in doing something good, usually by working hard

analysis n (p 70) the process of analysing something

Asia n (p 70) a continent

audience n (p 70) the people who sit and watch a performance at a theatre, cinema, etc.

conclusion n (p 73) the final part of something

convincing adj (p 69) able to make you believe that something is true or right

critic n (p 70) someone whose job is to give their opinion of a book, play, film, etc.

cultural adj (p 70) relating to the habits, traditions and beliefs of a society: *cultural diversity/identity*

culture n (p 70) music, art, theatre, literature, etc.

despite prep (p 70) used to say that something happened or is true, although something else makes this seem not probable: *I'm still pleased with the house despite all the problems we've had.*

dishonest adj (p 70) not honest and likely to lie or do something illegal

drama n (p 69) a play in a theatre or on television or radio: *a historical drama*

element n (p 71) a part of something: *This book has all the elements of a good detective story.*

entertainment n (p 70) shows, films, television, or other performances or activities that entertain people

era n (p 73) a period of time in history that is special for a particular reason: *the Victorian era*

genre n (p 70) a type of art or writing with a particular style

hero n (p 70) the main male character in a book or film who is usually good

influence n (p 70) the power to affect how someone thinks or behaves, or how something develops: *The drug companies have a lot of influence on doctors.*

interview n (p 70) a meeting in which someone is asked questions for a newspaper article, television show, etc.

journalist n (p 70) someone who writes news stories or articles for newspapers, magazines, television or radio

justify v (p 69) to give a good enough reason to make something seem acceptable

latest adj (p 71) most recent

originality n (p 70) the quality of being interesting and different from everyone or everything else

phenomenon n (p 70) something that exists or happens, usually something unusual: *Road rage seems to be a fairly recent phenomenon.*

plot n (p 69) the things that happen in a story

pretend v (p 70) *not pretend to be or do something* = not claim something that is false: *I don't pretend to be an expert on the subject.*

respect v (p 70) to admire someone because of their knowledge, achievements, etc.

scene n (p 69) a short part of a film, play, or book in which the events happen in one place: *the final scene*

scenery n (p 69) the large pictures of buildings, countryside, etc used on a theatre stage

simplify v (p 70) to make something less complicated or easier to do or to understand

star v (p 68) If a film, play, etc stars someone, or if someone stars in a film, play, etc, they are the main person in it.

steady adj (p 72) not changing: *She drove at a steady speed.*

teen n (p 69) teenager, someone who is between 13 and 19 years old

unique adj (p 70) unusual and special

valid adj (p 70) based on good reasons or facts that are true: *a valid argument*

values n (p 70) your beliefs about what is right and wrong and what is most important in life

villan n (p 70) a bad person in a film, book, etc.

UNIT 11 *The written word*

Describing books and journals

1 Label the parts of the book.

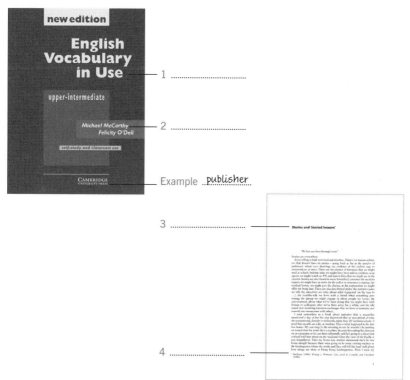

new edition

English Vocabulary in Use

upper-intermediate

Michael McCarthy
Felicity O'Dell

self-study and classroom use

CAMBRIDGE
UNIVERSITY PRESS

1 ....

2 ....

Example ..publisher..

3 ....

4 ....

2 Complete the sentences with a word from the box.

> bibliography   bestsellers   reviews   preface   paperback
> contents   glossary   blurb

1 Books usually come in hardback or .... versions.
2 Very popular books are known as ....
3 Some books have a ...., which is a kind of introduction.
4 You need to look in the table of .... to find out what
   the book contains.
5 Some academic books contain a .... , which explains
   difficult words, and a .... , which gives details of other
   works referred to.
6 Quotes from .... are often found on the back cover of a
   book. This is also known as the ....

VOCABULARY

45

Adverbs

1 **Fill the gaps in the account of an accident below, using the best adverbs from the box.**

> abruptly quite closely obviously seriously ~~casually~~
> certainly innocently fairly suddenly absolutely fast

I looked up from my magazine and glanced (example) ....*casually*....
out of the bus window, just in time to see the accident happen.
A small, silver car had entered the roundabout travelling rather
(1) .... A lorry, which was already on the
roundabout, stopped (2) .... in order to avoid
hitting the little car. There was a green Land Rover behind the lorry.
The driver of the Land Rover couldn't see what was happening in
front and so when the lorry driver (3) .... slammed
on his brakes, the Land Rover hit the back of the lorry. I don't think
the driver of the silver car even noticed. He (4) ....
didn't realise what he'd done because he continued on the
roundabout and proceeded (5) .... along the main
road. Luckily, nobody was (6) .... hurt but the
Land Rover was (7) .... badly damaged. The driver
was (8) .... furious.

Collocation

Adjectives and adverbs can be used to give more information about something
and to build up the length of sentences. For example 'a really exciting murder
mystery' is more helpful than 'a murder mystery'.
You must remember, though, that certain adverbs 'go with' certain adjectives.
This is called *collocation*.

2 **Here are seven well-known collocations that will help you in the Speaking test. Try to learn them by writing seven sentences about yourself and your interests.**

Example: Last night's documentary on wildlife was most informative.

1 rather dull
2 incredibly good
3 terribly exciting
4 extremely amusing
5 really interesting
6 totally relaxing
7 absolutely awful

Using adverbs and adjectives

1 Read the letter below and insert an adjective, adverb or both before the underlined words. Remember to change *a* to *an* where necessary.

Dear Sarah,

very exciting

I have just returned home from a|trip to Amsterdam in Holland.

I went there with my family for a <u>weekend</u>. We stayed in a <u>hotel</u>

in the centre of the city, which was <u>convenient</u>.

While we were there we visited the Van Gogh Museum. Van Gogh is

a <u>painter</u> and the museum was an <u>experience</u>. It has many of Van

Gogh's paintings on display and some of them are <u>moving</u>. I don't

think Van Gogh was always happy and this shows in his work. I

spent ages <u>looking</u> at the paintings and I bought some <u>prints</u>

before I left.

When I got home, I found some <u>frames</u> for the prints and now

they are hanging on my bedroom wall. I think Amsterdam will

always be a <u>place</u> for me.

Dong Xiang

Letter writing

2 Write a letter to someone about a museum that you have visited. Write three paragraphs that focus on

- where you went
- what you saw there
- how you felt about it.

Have you used adverbs and adjectives to improve your description? Check your letter for any grammatical errors.

WORD LIST

advantage *n* (p 77) something good about a situation that helps you: *One of the advantages of living in town is having the shops so near.*

adventurous *adj* (p 79) willing to try new and often difficult things

assess *v* (p 79) to make a judgment about the quality, size, value, etc. of something

colleague *n* (p 77) someone that you work with

comic *n* (p 74) a magazine with stories told in pictures

communication *n* (p 79) sharing information with others by speaking, writing, moving your body, or using other signals: *We can now communicate instantly with people on the other side of the world.*

disadvantage *n* (p 79) something which makes a situation more difficult, or makes you less likely to succeed

expect *v* (p 78) to think that someone should behave in a particular way or do a particular thing

gradually *adv* (p 77) slowly over a period of time

habit *n* (p 79) something that you do regularly, almost without thinking about it

imaginative *adj* (p 74) Something which is imaginative is new or clever and often unusual.

informative *adj* (p 74) containing a lot of useful facts

language *n* (p 75) a type of communication used by the people of a particular country: *How many languages do you speak?*

lastly *adv* (p 77) finally

lawyer *n* (p 74) someone whose job is to understand the law and deal with legal situations

library *n* (p 75) a room or building that contains a collection of books and other written material that you can read or borrow

literary *adj* (p 74) relating to literature, or typical of the type of language that is used in literature

novel *n* (p 75) a book that tells a story about imaginary people and events

otherwise *adv* (p 77) used after an order or suggestion to show what the result will be if you do not follow that order or suggestion: *I'd better write it down, otherwise I'll forget it.*

pause *v* (p 79) to stop doing something for a short time

press cutting *n* (p 74) a piece cut out of a newspaper

pronounce *v* (p 79) to make the sound of a letter or word: *How do you pronounce his name?*

proud *adj* (p 79) feeling very pleased about something you have done, something you own, or someone you know

rapid *adj* (p 76) happening or moving very quickly

realistic *adj* (p 74) showing things and people as they really are, or making them seem to be real

recommend *v* (p 78) to say that someone or something is good or suitable for a particular purpose: *Can you recommend a good book about animals for my son?*

relaxing *adj* (p 74) making you feel happy and comfortable because nothing is worrying you

romantic *adj* (p 75) relating to a story about love: *romantic fiction*

seem *v* (p 77) to appear to be a particular thing or to have a particular quality

straightforward *adj* (p 74) easy to understand or simple

stress *n* (p 77) feelings of worry caused by difficult situations such as problems at work

suggest *v* (p 78) to express an idea or plan for someone to consider

supportive *adj* (p 77) giving help or encouragement

technique *n* (p 75) a particular or special way of doing something

textbook *n* (p 74) a book about a particular subject, written for students

tired *adj* (p 75) feeling that you want to rest or sleep

usual *adj* (p 76) normal and happening most often

well-known *adj* (p 75) famous

Talking about rubbish

Complete each gap in the newspaper article below using a word that you have met on the first page of Unit 12.

Government gets involved in bag debate

ONE of the biggest issues facing our society today is the problem of how to (1) .... of our rubbish, and in particular, plastic bags, which cause serious damage to the (2) .... While these bags may last just an hour in your shopping basket, they take hundreds of years to break down. They choke up our rivers and (3) .... our waterways.

Some retailers have taken steps to (4) .... this from happening by introducing incentives to shoppers. For instance, one Byron Bay store is charging 10 cents a bag to customers to (5) .... them to bring their own bags.

In Ireland the government (6) .... a bag tax and plastic bag consumption went down by 90%. A study showed, however, that when they brought in this (7) ...., the sale of plastic bin liners immediately went up, which suggested that shoppers had been (8) .... their bags before by using them to line their rubbish bins. The government and the retail industry are now looking at other ways of (9) .... the use of plastic bags.

GRAMMAR

Verbs followed by prepositions

1 Complete the table by writing in the correct preposition. Use a dictionary to help you if necessary.

verb	preposition	
to stop someone	from	doing something
1 to protect someone		something
2 to dispose		something
3 to legislate		something
4 to involve someone		something
5 to apologise (to someone)		something
6 to approve		something
7 to argue (with someone)		something
8 to blame someone		something
9 to agree (with someone)		something
10 to believe		something
11 to decide		something
12 to rely		someone

2 Complete each sentence using a verb and preposition from exercise 1.

Example: These days we can ...protect....... children .....against..... most common diseases.

1 I would like to .... my bad behaviour.
2 I .... industry .... the pollution in our rivers.
3 I'm afraid I don't .... you. I think you're wrong.
4 I don't .... smoking. Apart from anything else, it's a fire hazard.
5 We .... all night .... whether we should cut down the forests. We are never going to agree.
6 The immigration authorities will .... you .... bringing any kind of food into Australia.
7 We need to get more people .... cleaning up the cities.
8 I really .... helping people but sometimes they have to help themselves too.

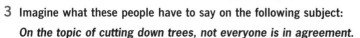

Balancing your views

1 Look at this picture of a forest and decide where you think it might be.

2 Write a paragraph about a forest you have been in and how you felt about it at the time.

3 Imagine what these people have to say on the following subject:

On the topic of cutting down trees, not everyone is in agreement.

Try to come up with three different points of view.

4 Write a paragraph balancing the views from exercise 3 which answers the question:

When, if ever, is it appropriate to cut down trees?

5 Read this paragraph, which answers the question in exercise 4, and fill each gap with a word or phrase from the box.

according to	from	I am concerned	on the other hand
prevent	provided that	so that	unfortunately

There seem to be different views on this topic, and these depend upon a number of factors. For example, people who enjoy walking in the forests would like to (1) .... people (2) .... cutting trees down. Also, we need trees for our oxygen, and, (3) .... conservationists, if we continue to cut them down, we will certainly destroy our planet.

(4) .... , people who make a living out of timber think they have a right to cut down trees. I think this is fine (5) .... they plant new trees to replace the ones they cut down. (6) .... , a lot of illegal logging also takes place and these trees are not replaced.

As far as (7) .... , the best approach would be to manage our forests more carefully (8) .... we only cut down trees when it helps other trees survive and remain healthy, or as part of a re-planting programme.

WRITING

WORD LIST

accept responsibility *v* (p 83) to say that you have done something or caused something to happen, especially something bad

anticipate *v* (p 81) to expect something, or to prepare for something before it happens

automobile *n* (p 82) a car

be to blame *v* (p 83) to be the main reason for something bad that happens: *The hot weather is partly to blame for the water shortage.*

campaign *n* (p 81) a series of organized activities or events intended to achieve a result: *an advertising campaign*

clear-cut *adj* (p 83) very certain or obvious

crop *n* (p 80) a plant such as a grain, fruit, or vegetable that is grown in large amounts by farmers

customs officer *n* (p 84) a person whose job is to look inside travellers' bags to make certain they are not taking goods into a country without paying taxes or carrying anything illegal

effectively *adv* (p 85) in a way that is successful and achieves what you want

encouragement *n* (p 80) when someone talks or behaves in a way that gives you confidence to do something

endangered *adj* (p 80) animals or plants which may soon not exist because there are very few now alive

environment *n* (p 84) the air, water, and land in or on which people, animals and plants live

event *n* (p 82) a race, party, competition, etc that has been organized for a particular time: *a social/sporting event*

fine *n* (p 83) an amount of money that you must pay for breaking a law or rule

genetically modified *adj* (p 80) describes a plant or animal that has had some of its genes changed scientifically

government *n* (p 80) the group of people who officially control a country

green *adj* (p 80) relating to nature and protecting the environment: *a green activist/campaigner*

heavy *adj* (p 83) large in amount or degree: *heavy costs*

import *v* (p 84) to bring something into your country from another country

instruction *n* (p 82) something that you have been told to do: *I had strict instructions to call them as soon as I arrived home.*

justifiable *adj* (p 84) having a good reason

legislate *v* (p 80) If a government legislates, it makes a new law.

legislation *n* (p 80) a law or a set of laws

management *n* (p 80) the control and organization of something

natural *adj* (p 84) as found in nature and not involving anything made or done by people

objective *n* (p 81) something that you are trying to achieve: *His main objective was to increase profits.*

politician *n* (p 82) someone who works in politics, especially a member of the government

prosecute *v* (p 83) to accuse someone of a crime in a law court

select *v* (p 82) to choose someone or something

species *n* (p 85) a group of plants or animals which share similar characteristics

stressed *adj* (p 80) when a word or syllable is pronounced with greater force than other words in the same sentence or other syllables in the same word

synonym *n* (p 82) a word or phrase that means the same as another word or phrase

tax *n* (p 84) money that you have to pay to the government from what you earn or when you buy things

wild *adj* (p 84) A wild animal or plant lives or grows in its natural environment and not where people live.

wooden *adj* (p 84) made of wood

Describing houses

1 Find some useful ways to describe a house or apartment in terms of these features:

	adjectives or phrases
material	concrete
age	
cost	
appearance	
location	
style	

Crossword

2 Complete the puzzle. You met most of these words in Unit 13.

Across

1 It protects you from the wind and rain. (7)
4 He works with wood. (9)
5 They'll keep your house out of the water. (6)
8 This material has replaced bricks and stone. (8)
10 It separates you from your neighbours. (4)
11 another word for an apartment (4)

Down

1 They'll lead you up or down. (6)
2 This person rents a house. (6)
3 This person designs buildings. (9)
6 A key turns a .... (4)
7 a very strong building material (5)
9 This makes *6 down* work more smoothly. (3)

GRAMMAR

Linking and reference words

1 Read the following description of a home. Try to improve it by replacing
some of the nouns with a pronoun and by linking the sentences. Use the
words in the margin to help you.

The house where I grew up

The house I grew up in was in the old part of Singapore. The house was some distance from the city centre and had an interesting history. It belonged to an old lady. The lady lived next door with her daughter and grandchildren. Her family had owned it since before the war. My parents rented the house from this lady. The lady was always very kind to me.	it who her and she
The house was made of solid brick and had a little garden. It looked out on the jungle. This was unusual. The traditional Singaporean house is made of wood, and often stands on stilts to protect it from the floods. Floods regularly occur in the rainy season.	which as which
Last year I returned to Singapore in the hope of finding the house again. I could not find the house. Perhaps it has been pulled down to make way for the modern high-rise buildings. High rise buildings now predominate on the island. I suppose that is a sign of the times.	but it which

---

Expressing purpose with 'in order to'

In order to is useful in more formal writing to express the link between an action and a purpose. The negative form is *in order not to*. You can begin your sentence with the expression, or you can use it in the middle of a sentence to link the two ideas. Both are correct.

2 Link the following ideas twice, using *in order to* in both positions.
Change the wording as necessary.

Example: Students want a refund. They must inform the college in writing.
Students must inform the college in writing, in order to receive a refund.
In order to receive a refund, students must inform the college in writing.

1 Students want to be successful. They must be able to work alone.
2 You want to meet the deadline. You need to hand in your work by October 10th.
3 Governments set up advertising campaigns. They encourage people to be more environmentally aware.
4 Consumers don't want to spend too much time shopping. They make quick purchasing decisions.
5 The director spoke very softly. He wanted to make people listen carefully.
6 I needed to improve my Spanish quickly. I joined an intensive evening class.

Making a concession

Look at the numbered notes in columns A and B below. Column A contains a topic with two opposing points of view. Column B reinforces one of these viewpoints.

▶ Use the notes in column A to make a statement and a concession like this:

While mobile phones are expensive, for some people they have become essential for communication.

▶ Then use the notes in column B to support the argument. The point of view in column B should be the 'winning' argument. Try to use an appropriate linking word or phrase.

Example:

While mobile phones are expensive, for some people they have become essential for communication. I think that in particular they are useful in emergencies, and they allow children to be in contact with their parents at any time.

	A	B
	Mobile phones: expensive but essential for communication	useful in emergencies / for children to contact parents
1	Dogs: unhygienic but good pets	Domestic dogs don't belong in the city
2	Students living at home: not independent but economical	Young people / need to be independent / make their own way
3	Old buildings: historical interest but impractical	Important link to the past / belong to everyone
4	Horse-racing: provides entertainment and taxes for the government, but people over-spend	Government should not encourage legal gambling / people may borrow money and get into debt / tax luxury goods
5	Fashionable clothes: waste of money but look good	People are 'slaves to fashion' / influenced by magazines and advertising

Unit 13 Safe as houses

argument *n* (p 90) a reason or reasons why you support or oppose an idea or suggestion, or the process of explaining them

artistic *adj* (p 87) relating to art

balanced *adj* (p 89) considering all the facts in a fair way

belong *v* (p 86) to be in the right or suitable place

civic *adj* (p 88) relating to a city or town and the people who live there

consequence *n* (p 90) the result of an action or situation, especially a bad result

create *v* (p 90) to make something happen or exist

department *n* (p 90) a part of an organization such as a school, business, or government which deals with a particular area of work

determine *v* (p 87) to decide what will happen: *Her exam results will determine which university she goes to.*

educated *adj* (p 91) Someone who is educated has learned a lot at school or university and has a good level of knowledge.

heritage *n* (p 90) the buildings, paintings, customs, etc. which are important in a culture or society because they have existed for a long time

impersonal *adj* (p 87) lacking human warmth and interest

impress *v* (p 88) to make someone admire or respect you

impressive *adj* (p 88) Someone or something that is impressive makes you admire and respect them.

justify *v* (p 89) to give a good enough reason to make something seem acceptable

knowledge *n* (p 90) information and understanding that you have in your mind

lecture *n* (p 86) a formal talk given to a group of people in order to teach them about a subject

major *adj* (p 91) more important or more serious that other things or people of a similar type: *a major problem, to play a major role in something*

point *n* (p 90) purpose or usefulness: *There's no point inviting her – she never comes to parties.*

practical *adj* (p 87) suitable for the situation in which something is used: *I tend to wear clothes that are practical rather than fashionable.*

preserve *v* (p 90) to keep something the same or prevent it from being destroyed

principle *n* (p 87) a basic idea or rule which explains how something happens or works

reader *n* (p 91) someone who reads

reflect *v* (p 89) to show or be a sign of something: *The statistics reflect a change in people's spending habits.*

require *v* (p 91) to need or demand something

responsible *adj* (p 89) to be responsible for something to be the person who caused something to happen, especially something bad: *Who was responsible for the accident?*

suggestion *n* (p 88) an idea or plan that someone suggests

ugly *adj* (p 88) unpleasant to look at

valuable *adj* (p 90) Valuable objects could be sold for a lot of money.

VOCABULARY

Adjective formation

There are many words that are used to express feelings, views and opinions. Look at how the adjective *unexciting* is formed by adding *un-* at the start and replacing the *-e* with *-ing* at the end.

from *excite* (verb)

↓

un- prefix ⟶ un<u>exciting</u> ⟵ *-ing* suffix

1 Complete the sentences by forming a word to fill each gap. Remember that you will not always need a prefix and sometimes you may have to change the ending of the original word. Check your spelling afterwards.

prefix	stem	suffix
	consider	
	convince	
	delight	
	doubt	able
	exhaust	ant
dis	help	ate
in	health	ed
un	memory	ful
	optimist	ic
	please	ing
	respect	ory
	reward	y
	satisfy	
	sympathy	

1 I always look on the bright side, so I'm very .... about the future.

2 People who puff cigarette smoke in your face are just totally ....

3 I was .... to hear that I had finally got a place at my chosen university.

4 We should try to avoid eating a lot of .... food, such as chips.

5 The firefighters do a valuable job, so I'm .... towards their claims for higher pay.

6 I keep thinking back to my graduation – it was such a .... occasion.

2 Complete the sentences using a word related to the word **in italics.**

Example: I am *convinced by* this argument. It is a ..*convincing*.. argument.

1 I have *doubts* about this theory. I am .... about this theory.

2 Other scientists *respect* Ekman's work. Ekman is a .... scientist.

3 I get *exhausted* being a nurse. Nursing is an .... profession.

4 I am not *satisfied* with this solution. This is not a .... solution.

5 Some people's attitude doesn't *help*. Some people have an .... attitude.

6 The task isn't very *pleasant*. It's an .... task.

7 People say that teachers get many *rewards* from their work. Teaching is considered to be a .... career.

Phrasal verbs

1 Look at this extract from the recording script in Unit 14 and the definition from the *Cambridge International Dictionary of Phrasal Verbs*.

> I'll probably get up in the middle of the night and start practising.

get up gets, getting, got (*American pp* also **gotten**)

get (sb) **up**
  to wake up and get out of bed, or to make someone do this • *I had to get up at five o'clock this morning* • *Can you get the kids up?*

Underline the phrasal verb(s) in these extracts.

1 I felt really let down after all my efforts.

2 Tom and I are really looking forward to going away for a couple of weeks.

3 ... I'm not very good at choosing clothes. I tend to go for things that don't match ...

4 It's been such a difficult time for me catching up with all the work I missed ...

5 ... we're supposed to come up with all sorts of arguments about why we think animal testing is right or wrong ...

6 Samil, I was just wondering why you decided not to take up that job offer in Germany?

7 You said before the interview that it might not be the right kind of position for you ... was that your reason for turning the job down ...?

8 They turned up over an hour late.

9 I don't know where he's going with it (the car) but there's something going on.

2 Replace the words *in italics* with one of the phrasal verbs from exercise 1.

1 I think I'll *accept* my friend's advice and look for a new apartment.
2 Peter tends to *choose* classical music.
3 I promised to help Katy do her assignment so I mustn't *disappoint her*.
4 To my surprise, some of the audience *arrived* half way through the concert.
5 Brian said he would marry Helen and take her to Japan with him but she still *refused him*.
6 We're all *pleased to be going to* Pam's birthday meal next week.
7 Mr Timms expects us to talk in the seminar tomorrow but I can't *think of* any original ideas.
8 I wish somebody would tell me what's *happening*!

Describing what people do

In the IELTS test, you will read passages from different study areas. Often they have been written by specialists and they include references to academic experts. It is important to be aware of the different subjects that you might meet.

1 Scan the passage on pages 94 and 95 of your Student's Book for people's names and complete the table below.

name	job
Paul Ekman	psychologist

2 Complete the table.

person	area of work or study	person	area of work or study
agriculturalist	agriculture		geology
anthropologist		journalist	
archaeologist		linguist	
	architecture		nutrition
	economics	philosopher	
educationalist		psychologist	
environmentalist			zoology

3 Write a sentence about what each of the following people do.

Example: *A philosopher studies ideas and knowledge in an attempt to understand the world better.*

1 An educationalist ....
2 A psychologist ....
3 A geologist ....
4 An environmentalist ....
5 A linguist ....
6 A journalist ....

4 Which area of study or discipline do you associate with the following pictures? Write a sentence that explains what each one is.

Example: *Agriculture is the study of farming and farming methods.*

59

WORD LIST

ability *n* (p 95) the physical or mental skill or qualities that you need to do something

anxious *adj* (p 92) worried and nervous

check *v* (p 95) to examine something in order to make sure that it is correct or the way it should be

collection *n* (p 95) a group of objects of the same type that have been collected by one person or in one place

combination *n* (p 95) arrangement of two or more things in a different order

complex *adj* (p 94) involving a lot of different but connected parts in a way that is difficult to understand: *The situation is very complex.*

concentrate *v* (p 95) to think very carefully about something you are doing and nothing else

disappointed *adj* (p 93) unhappy because someone or something was not as good as you hoped or expected

discover *v* (p 94) to get information about something for the first time: *She discovered that he had been married three times before.*

discuss *v* (p 93) to talk about something with someone and tell each other your ideas or opinions

distinguish *v* (p 94) to recognize the differences between two people, ideas, or things

efficient *adj* (p 94) working well and not wasting time or energy

emotion *n* (p 95) a strong feeling such as love or anger, or strong feelings in general

establish *v* (p 95) to find out information or prove something

explanation *n* (p 95) the details or reasons that someone gives to make something clear or easy to understand

factor *n* (p 96) one of the things that has an effect on a particular situation, decision, event, etc: *Money was an important factor in their decision to move.*

fairly *adv* (p 92) more than average, but less than very: *a fairly big family*

fictional *adj* (p 97) existing only in fiction

fundamental *adj* (p 94) relating to the most important or main part of something: *a fundamental change/difference*

guest *n* (p 97) someone who comes to visit you in your home, at a party, etc.

instrument *n* (p 94) someone or something that is used for achieving something: *The Internet is a very powerful instrument of communication.*

interpret *v* (p 94) to explain or decide what you think a particular phrase, performance, action, etc. means

judgement *n* (p 95) an opinion about someone or something that you decide on after thinking carefully

marriage *n* (p 93) the legal relationship of a man and a woman being a husband and a wife

married *adj* get married *v* (p 93) to begin a legal relationship with someone as their husband or wife

memorable *adj* (p 94) If an occasion is memorable, you will remember it for a long time because it is so good.

movement *n* (p 95) a change of position or place

name *v* (p 94) to give someone or something a name: *A young boy named Peter answered the phone.*

normal *adj* (p 94) usual, ordinary, and expected

photograph *n* (p 94) a picture produced with a camera

precise *adj* (p 92) exact and accurate

recommendation *n* (p 92) a piece of advice about what to do in a particular situation: *It's my recommendation that this factory be closed immediately.*

scientific *adj* (p 94) relating to science, or using the organized methods of science

scientist *n* (p 94) someone who studies science or works in science

sort *v* (p 95) to arrange things into different groups or types or into an order

teenage *adj* (p 92) aged between 13 and 19 or suitable for people of that age

typical *adj* (p 97) having all the qualities you expect a particular person, object, place, etc. to have: *typical German food*

universal *adj* (p 94) relating to everyone in the world, or to everyone in a particular group

wedding *n* (p 97) an official ceremony at which a man and woman get married

Abbreviations

1 You may come across these abbreviations or signs in the IELTS test. What do they stand for?

Abbreviation	Meaning
Example: IQ	_Intelligence Quotient_ (measure of how intelligent someone is)
1 AI	Artificial ....
2 OPEC	Organisation of ....
3 GDP	Gross ....
4 EU	European ....
5 co	....
6 km	....
7 kg	....
8 A$	....
9 £	....
10 %	....
11 bn	....

Reference word plus noun formation

2 Complete the sentences using a reference word + the correct form of the word in brackets.

Example: I think hospital workers, fire fighters and carers are the most important people in society. ...These professionals... (profession) work very hard for all of us.

1 It is important to think about price and quality when buying food. .... (consider) are more important than quantity.

2 People are beginning to see that they need to do more to reduce traffic congestion. However, ... (realise) is occurring quite slowly.

3 It is certainly true that we rely heavily on computers and .... (depend) is likely to continue.

4 Walking, swimming and cycling are very good for you. You should stay fit if you regularly take part in one of .... (active).

5 The train to London was two hours late yesterday. Unfortunately .... (delay) are not uncommon.

6 It has been suggested that computers should be banned because they are dangerous to health. .... (suggest) can only be described as short-sighted.

GRAMMAR

The future

Complete the conversations using the verb in brackets in an appropriate form.

When would you expect me to start work at your company?

Well, our next project _is starting_ (start) in three weeks' time, so we _would need_ (need) to have you here by then.

1

Let's go out for a drink tonight!

I'm afraid I can't. I .... (take) my grandmother to the theatre.

2

If any more staff go sick this week, the factory .... (definitely/close).

Don't worry. I'm sure they .... (be) back tomorrow.

3

I think I .... (like) to see you again in about two weeks' time.

OK, I .... (go) on holiday next week but I .... (be) free the following week – I'll just check my diary.

4

You know I .... (do) anything for you!

Mmm. .... (you/still/say) that in ten years' time, I wonder?

5

If I wore the same colour as you every day, how .... (you/feel)?

I think I .... (feel) rather irritated!

Checking for reference and tense error

1 Read the essay below, which is an answer to the following task:

Some people argue that technology has had a positive influence on the music industry because it allows people to show their musical talents without having to play a musical instrument. Others argue that you need to be able to play an instrument in order to prove that you are really talented.

Discuss both these views.

The answer contains 11 errors in tenses or referencing. The first one has been identified. Can you find the others and correct them?

> Pronoun not needed after 'something'.

In my view, musical talent is something that is hard to define it. If you are good at the piano or the violin do these mean that you have musical talent? Or is it just that you had to play these instruments as a child? You have the skill, perhaps, but not necessarily the talent. The question of whether such a technology is a good influence is difficult because it may help people which aren't able to have music lessons. In my case, I have learnt the flute when I was young but I don't play now. It is because I was never really interested – my parents just forced me to do it. However, I have a friend who can't play any instruments, but he's a very good composer on the synthesiser. He also uses PC software to record her songs. In my opinion, he has a lot more musical talent than I do. As far as commercial music is concerned, I think my view is a little different. In the pop world, for instance, a lot of people become famous recently without having much talent. If you have a good singing voice and you are attractive then it's possible that you could be successful. Such outcome doesn't really seem right. I think you should still have something outstanding to become famous. All in all, I think musical talent does exist, but I am strongly believe that some people have it while others do not. For this, I don't really think that technology has anything to do with it. People such as my friend prove to me that talent is still the most important factor.

2 The writer has forgotten to paragraph this essay. Mark the essay where you think any new paragraphs should start.

3 The writer has used a number of words and expressions to show how his or her argument links together. Find examples of the following:

1 introducing a new idea ....

2 summing up an argument ....

3 contrasting ....

4 adding a supporting point ....

5 exemplifying a point ....

6 giving a personal view ....

affect v (p 102) to influence someone or something, or cause them to change: *It's a disease which affects many older people.*

apparently adv (p 100) used to say that you have read or been told something although you are not certain it is true: *Apparently it's going to rain today.*

approach v (p 99) to deal with something: *I'm not sure how to approach the problem.*

argue v (p 98) to give reasons to support or oppose an idea, action, etc: *He argued that cuts in military spending were necessary.*

artificial adj (p 98) not natural, but made by people

business n (p 101) an organization that sells goods or services

celebrate v (p 102) to do something enjoyable because it is a special day, or because something good has happened

complaint n (p 101) when someone says that something is wrong or not satisfactory

construct v (p 98) to build something from several parts

cope v (p 98) to deal quite successfully with a difficult situation

correspondence n (p 101) letters from one person to another, or the activity of writing and receiving letters

dedicated adj (p 98) designed to be used for a particular purpose

develop v (p 98) to grow or change and become more advanced, or to make someone or something do this: *She's taking a course to develop her computer skills.*

domestic adj (p 98) relating to the home and family relationships

dominate v (p 101) to control or have power over someone or something

error n (p 98) a mistake, especially one that can cause problems

exhibition n (p 100) when objects such as paintings are shown to the public

expert system n (p 98) a computer system which asks questions and gives answers that have been thought of by a human expert

foresee v (p 102) to expect a future situation or event

gradual adj (p 100) happening slowly over a period of time

hopefully adv (p 101) used, often at the start of a sentence, to express what you would like to happen: *Hopefully it won't rain.*

intelligence n (p 98) the ability to learn, understand, and think about things

inventor n (p 98) someone who designs and makes new things

involve v (p 98) If a situation or activity involves something, that thing is a necessary part of it: *The trips often involve a lot of walking.*

lengthen v (p 102) to become longer or to make something longer

lifespan n (p 102) the amount of time that a person lives or a thing exists

logical adj (p 98) using reason: *a logical choice/conclusion*

manufacture v (p 98) to produce something, usually in large numbers in a factory

predict v (p 102) to say what you think will happen in the future

prediction n (p 102) when you say what you think will happen in the future

process n (p 98) a method of producing goods in a factory

refer v (p 99) to talk or write about someone or something, especially briefly

robot n (p 98) a machine controlled by a computer, which can move and do other things that people can do

search engine n (p 98) a computer program which finds information on the Internet by looking for words which you have typed in

slight adj (p 100) small and not important: *slight differences in colour*

speculate v (p 102) to guess possible answers to a question when you do not have enough information to be certain: *The newspapers have speculated that they will get married next year.*

surely adv (p 98) used to express that you are certain or almost certain about something: *Without more food and medical supplies, these people will surely not survive.*

transform v (p 101) to change something completely, usually to improve it

workplace n (p 101) the place where you work

UNIT 16 Mother tongue

Word puzzle

1 Complete the word puzzle and find the word in the tinted squares.

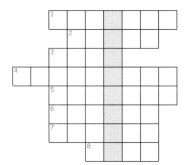

Clues

1 local version of a language
2 This organ controls your body and mind.
3 something to show you the way
4 able to speak two languages
5 You will get these after the exam.
6 official argument or discussion
7 Your native language is your mother ....
8 unable to hear

Singular and plural meanings

2 Complete the following sentences with the appropriate singular or plural form of the noun in brackets.

Example: a I enjoy going to the cinema but I much prefer live ....*theatre*.... .

b There are hundreds of ....*theatres*.... in London. (theatre)

1 a My grandfather could speak four .... (language)
   b Human beings are not the only creatures to have developed ....

2 a There are many .... for learning (reason)
      a second language.
   b Children under three are too young to understand ....

3 a The .... of competition at the (standard)
      Olympic Games is always high.
   b In teaching, it is important to ensure high .... in the classroom.

4 a When I was young, I was always having (argument)
      .... with my sisters.
   b You need to present a well-supported .... in your essay for this exam.

5 a Humans are the only animals to have (speech)
      developed ....
   b I'm not very good at making .... in public.

6 a Hinduism and Buddhism are ancient (religion)
      .... of the East.
   b For many people, ... is a central part of their lives.

GRAMMAR

Adverbs ending in -ly

1 **Use an appropriate adverb from the box to replace the <u>underlined</u> words.**

Example: I like receiving e-mails but I'm <u>just as</u> happy to get a letter
in the mail. *equally*

| hopefully | unfortunately | usually | frankly | ~~equally~~ |
| luckily | occasionally | coincidentally | normally | |

1 <u>Under normal circumstances</u> I come to the university each day.

2 <u>Most days</u> I attend lectures from 9 to 12 every morning.

3 <u>From time to time</u> I have to miss my Tuesday lectures because of my
   part-time job.

4 <u>I'm sorry to say</u> I won't be able continue my studies next year because
   I have to leave the country.

5 <u>With a bit of luck,</u> I'll be able to continue my studies next year but it's
   not certain.

6 I was whistling a song when I turned on the radio and, <u>would you
   believe it</u>, they were playing the same song.

7 I missed the bus this morning but then, <u>thank goodness</u>, my neighbour
   gave me a lift to the university.

8 <u>To be honest,</u> I don't really like London. I think it's too busy and
   crowded.

Indirect questions

2 **Turn the following direct questions into indirect questions using *if* or
whether. Remember to use the same tense as the verb in the question.**

Examples: Are we too late to get into the movie?
*Can you tell me / Can you say if/whether we're too late to get into the
film?*

Did the medical supplies arrive on time?
Do you know if/whether the medical supplies arrived on time?

1 Are you going to the Economics lecture today?
2 Does the postman deliver the mail before mid-day?
3 Did my client leave a message for me at the reception desk?
4 Will you be coming back to the office this afternoon?
5 Is Susan in the library or the cafeteria?
6 Have you got an exam this week?
7 Does your brother want to live in student accommodation next year?
8 Has the writer answered the question?
9 Are the Johnsons coming for dinner tonight, or not?
10 Did anybody feed the dog?

Linking words

1 Look at this Task 2 writing question and rephrase the quote in your own words.

A report written in the 1960s made the following claim: "Machine translation (MT) is slower and less accurate than human translation and there is no immediate or predictable likelihood of machines taking over this role from humans."

To what extent do you think this is still true today?
Could a machine ever take the place of a human translator or interpreter?

2 Now read the answer below and complete it by choosing an appropriate expression from the list of linking words below to fill gaps 1–13.

(Example) ...It is true.. that there have been <u>great advances in technology over the last forty years</u>. ....(1) .... the use of mobile phones and e-mail communication are common these days. ....(2) ...., machines which translate from one language to another are still in their early stages.

....(3) .... that a machine could never do as good a job as a human, ...(4) .... when it comes to interpreting what people are saying. ....(5) ...., machines can translate statements such as 'Where is the bank?' but even simple statements are not always straightforward ....(6) .... meaning depends on more than just words. ....(7) .... the word 'bank' has a number of different meanings in English. How does a translating machine know which meaning to take?

....(8) .... understand what people are saying, you need to take into account the relationship between the speakers and their situation. A machine cannot tell the difference between the English expression 'Look out!' meaning 'Be careful! and 'Look out!' meaning 'Put your head out of the window'. You need a human being to interpret the situation.

....(9) .... with written language, it is difficult for a machine to know how to translate accurately ....(10) .... we rarely translate every word. ....(11) ...., we try to take into consideration how the idea would be expressed in the other language. This is hard to do ....(12) .... every language has its own way of doing and saying things.

....(13) .... I feel that it is most unlikely that machines will take the place of humans in the field of translation and interpreting. If machines ever learn to think, perhaps then they will be in a position to take on this role.

for example	it seems to me	however	similarly
of course	it is true	in order to	for these reasons
because	especially	for instance	on the contrary

Main ideas

3 Underline the main idea in each paragraph and write it in your own words.

WORD LIST

academy n (p 106) an organization whose purpose is to encourage and develop an art, science, language, etc.

certainty n (p 111) when you are completely sure about something: *I can't say with any certainty what time she left.*

chemical adj (p 107) relating to chemistry or chemicals

clarify v (p 111) to make something easier to understand by explaining it

confirm v (p 106) to say or show that something is true: *His wife confirmed that he'd left the house at 8.*

convey v (p 110) to communicate information, feelings, or images to someone

define v (p 107) to say exactly what something means, or what someone or something is like: *Can you define what it means to be an American?*

dependence n (p 111) when you need someone or something all the time in order to exist or continue as before

disruption n (p 109) when something, especially a system, process or event, is prevented from continuing as usual or as expected

distinction n (p 106) a difference between two similar things: *the distinction between spoken and written language*

encyclopedia n (p 106) a book or a set of books containing facts about a lot of subjects

existence n (p 106) when something or someone exists

fascinating adj (p 106) extremely interesting

fruitless adj (p 106) not successful or achieving good results

illuminate v (p 110) to explain something clearly or make it easier to understand

initial adj (p 111) first, or happening at the beginning

investigate v (p 107) to try to discover all the facts about something, especially a crime or accident

literacy n (p 105) the ability to read and write

minority n (p 106) any small group in society that is different from the rest because of their race, religion, or political beliefs

mistaken adj (p 109) wrong in what you believe, or based on a belief that is wrong

mutually adv (p 110) You use mutually before an adjective when the adjective describes all sides of a situation: *a mutually dependent relationship; Being attractive and intelligent are not mutually exclusive* (= someone can be attractive and intelligent).

nationality n (p 104) If you have American/British/Swiss, etc. nationality, you are legally a member of that country.

native adj (p 104) Your native language is the first language you learn.

origin n (p 107) the cause of something, or where something begins or comes from: *the origin of the universe*

policy n (p 106) a set of ideas or a plan of what to do in particular situations that has been agreed by a government, business, etc: *economic policy*

potential n (p 111) qualities or abilities that may develop and allow someone or something to succeed: *She has a lot of potential as a writer.*

proficiency n (p 110) when you can do something very well: *The job requires proficiency in written and spoken English.*

recognise v (p 107) to accept that something is true or real: *She recognised that she had been partly to blame.*

regional adj (p 106) relating to a region (= particular area in a country)

relevance n (p 111) the degree to which something is related or useful to what is happening or being talked about: *This point has no relevance to the discussion.*

restrict v (p 108) to limit something

roughly adv (p 104) approximately

severe adj (p 109) extremely bad

shape n (p 110) the physical form of something made by the line around its outer edge: *a circular/rectangular shape*

spatial adj (p 109) relating to the position, area, and size of things

structure v (p 109) to arrange something in an organized way

systematic adj (p 110) done using a fixed and organized plan

tend v (p 109) to often do a particular thing or be likely to do a particular thing

thought n (p 108) an idea or opinion

tradition n (p 106) a belief, principle or way of behaving that has continued for a long time in a group of people or a society

uncertainty n (p 106) the state of not knowing what to do or believe, or not being able to decide about something

visual adj (p 109) relating to seeing

vocal adj (p 110) involving or relating to the voice, especially singing

Acknowledgements

The authors and publishers are grateful to the following for permission to use copyright material in *Step Up to IELTS Personal Study Book*. While every effort has been made, it has not been possible to identify the sources of all the material used and in such cases the publishers would welcome information from the copyright owners:

For p. 19, the facts about Australia taken from *Living World Geography* by B & J Parker, published by Macmillan Education Australia; for the graph on p. 26, 'From acorn to oak', *The Economist*, June 2nd 2001, and for the graph on p. 27, 'Down, but levelling off', *The Economist*, May 25th 2002, and for the graph, 'High-budget films', *The Economist*, March 29th 2001 (from the article 'A fine romance'), and for the graph on p. 27, 'The cost of progress', *The Economist*, July 14th 2001, and for the graph on p. 27, 'Not a pretty picture', *The Economist*, February 3rd 2001, and for the graph on p. 27, 'Cleaning up' (from the article 'The truth about the environment), *The Economist*, August 2nd 2001, © The Economist Newspaper Limited, London; for the extract on p. 49, 'Government gets involved in bag debate', with kind permission of Clean Up Australia/Clean Up the World © Clean Up Australia 2000. http://www.cleanup.com.au.

The definitions in this book are based on those in *Cambridge Learner's Dictionary* and *Cambridge Advanced Learner's Dictionary* (Cambridge University Press). For more information about the learners' dictionaries published by Cambridge, visit our dictionary website at http://dictionary.cambridge.org